D1178770

THE DISCIPLE'S HANDBOOK

The Disciple's Handbook

One Merrill Street
Woburn, MA 01801
1-888-DPI-BOOK • FAX (781) 937-3889
www.dpibooks.com

All Scripture quotations, unless indicated, are taken from the
HOLY BIBLE, NEW INTERNATIONAL VERSION.
Copyright @ 1973, 1978, 1984 by the International Bible Society.
Used by permission of Zondervan Publishing House.
All rights reserved.

The "NIV" and "New International Version" trademarks
are registered in the United States Patent Trademark Office
by the International Bible Society.
Use of either trademarks requires the permission
of the International Bible Society.

The Disciple's Handbook

© 1997 by Discipleship Publications International
One Merrill Street, Woburn, MA 01801

All rights reserved. No part of this book may be
duplicated, copied, translated, reproduced or stored
mechanically or electronically without specific,
written permission of
Discipleship Publications International.

Exceptions to this are noted on page 178
where permission is granted to reproduce certain pages
when such reproduction will not result in sales of the copies.

Printed in the United States of America

Edited by: Thomas A. Jones
Book design: Chris Costello

ISBN 1-57782-033-9

Contents

Part Three: Ideas

Part Four: Planning and Evaluation

Introduction

This volume represents an effort to bring together in one place a number of items that will help disciples who are studying the Bible with others, discipling young Christians, and seeking ways to be of greater service to God. Information found here ranges from studies in various situations to songs for use in family devotionals.

Perhaps the most interesting section is Part Four where the reader will find some unique direction in evaluating his or her life and making plans for the future.

May God bless you as you use this material to bring others to him and to help them and yourself to grow.

PART ONE

•Studies•

First Principles

Basic Studies for Making Disciples

INTRODUCTION

The *First Principles* studies are taught around the world addressing the challenges to faith and doctrine in each culture. Kip McKean prepared this study series in 1979 with two purposes in mind: (1) to bring non-believers into a saving relationship with Jesus Christ, and (2) to provide a basis for the new Christian to fulfill the Great Commission by "making disciples."

Through the years the series has been fine-tuned to meet specific needs. Section One provides a foundation in Christ that can be built on for a lifetime. These first twelve lessons also prepare a person to make a decision of total commitment to Christ and to his kingdom and to celebrate the results. Section Two, prepared in 1989 by Kip McKean, contains four follow-up studies which clarify the Christian's role in this world. Not only do these studies provide content for several discipleship times, but they also help provide a smooth transition from the *First Principles* studies into a discipling relationship.

by Kip McKean
Edited by Steven Zedler
and Leigh Ann Hooper Vett

Discipleship

Introduction: Matthew 28:18-20

A. What does Jesus want everybody to become?

B. Which is the more popular term—disciple or Christian?

C. The word "Christian" only appears three times in the New Testament. It was the name those in the world gave the disciples (Acts 11:19-26), seven years after the church began.

D. The word "disciple" occurs over 270 times in the New Testament. Jesus defines the term disciple throughout his ministry.

E. Jesus came to make disciples. Only disciples will be saved.

1. Mark 1:14-18

A. Calling of the first disciples

B. Come follow me (Christ).

C. "...make you fishers of men"—Jesus gave these first disciples the real purpose for living.

D. Immediately

2. Luke 9:23-26

A. If any man...

B. Deny self. Notice Christ in the garden (Matthew 26:36-39, "Not my will, but your will.") Don't give in to moods.

C. Carry the cross—daily.

D. Gain world ... forfeit soul. Lose your life for Jesus ... save it.

3. Luke 14:25-33

A. If any man...

B. Count the cost (vv. 28-30).

C. Consider the alternatives (vv. 31-32).

D. Love Christ more than any person (v. 26).

E. Persecutions (v. 27)

F. Everything, not just anything (v. 33)

4. Luke 11:1-4

A. Must learn to pray—disciples saw the strength Jesus received from the Father.

B. Daily personal relationship with God (v. 3)

5. John 13:34-35

A. Love one another.

B. Be an active part of the fellowship.

6. Matthew 28:18-20

A. Command—make disciples (given to all)

B. Who is a candidate for baptism? Disciples

C. You need someone to disciple you to maturity in Christ.

D. This is the only way to save the world!

Year	Preacher	Discipler
1	365	2
2	730	4
3	1095	8
13	4,745	8,192
32	11,680	the world, 5 billion plus

Concluding Questions

A. Am I a disciple?

B. Am I a Christian?

C. Am I saved?

D. What do I need to do to become a disciple?

The Word of God

1. 2 Timothy 3:16-17
   A. All Scripture is inspired by God.
   B. It is to be applied to our lives.

2. Hebrews 4:12-13
   A. The Word is relevant.
   B. The Word cuts (hurts)—compare it to a scalpel.
   C. It is good to be cut because the scalpel cuts the "cancer" (sin) out.

3. 2 Peter 1:20-21
   A. There is no private interpretation of the Bible.
   B. The Holy Spirit inspired the men who wrote the books of the Bible.

4. John 8:31-32
   A. Intellectual belief is not enough—nor can we go by our feelings.
   B. Everyone must hold on to and follow the teachings of Jesus to be a true disciple.
   C. Sincerity does not equal truth.
   D. Religious people can be wrong.

5. Matthew 15:1-9
   A. Do not go by traditions or creeds.
   B. Worship by traditions (which supersede the word of God) is worship in vain.

6. 1 Timothy 4:16
   A. Watch your life and doctrine closely—they are inseparable.
   B. Which is more important, life or doctrine? Neither—an airplane with only one wing cannot fly.
   C. Why is it so important to learn and to teach and to live the right doctrine? To save yourself and those who hear you.

7. Acts 17:10-12
   A. You must check what religious leaders say.
   B. Your challenge: Read and study the Bible every day!

8. John 12:48
   A. Why study the Bible? The Word will judge us.
   B. Decision: Will I live by the Bible or my feelings, traditions, needs, etc.?

NOTES:

The Coming of the Kingdom

Importance of this study:

A. Produce faith in the continuity of the Word.

B. Kingdom is the church—importance of the church in the eternal plan of God.

1. Old Testament predictions of the Kingdom (The height of Israel's glory was under the kingship of David approximately 1000 B.C.)
   A. Isaiah 2:1-4 (750 B.C.)
      1) Last days
      2) All nations
      3) Jerusalem
   B. Daniel 2:44, 7:18 (550 B.C.)
      1) Endure forever
      2) Possess forever

2. New Testament predictions of the Kingdom
   A. John the Baptist (25 A.D.) Kingdom is near (Matthew 3:1-6)
   B. Jesus (30 A.D.)
      1) Kingdom is near (Matthew 4:17)
      2) Kingdom will come in the lifetime of some of the disciples (Mark 9:1)
      3) Kingdom will come with power (Mark 9:1)
      4) Kingdom entered by new birth (John 3:1-7)
      5) Kingdom is within you (Luke 17:20-21)
      6) Peter has the keys (Matthew 16:13-19). Church and the Kingdom are the same and will be built on the truth that Jesus is the Christ (1 Corinthians 3:11).
      7) Joseph of Arimathea was still waiting for the Kingdom when Jesus died (Luke 23:50-51).
      8) Repentance and forgiveness of sins will be preached first in Jerusalem to all nations (Luke 24:44-49).

3. Fulfillment of the Old and New Testament predictions (Acts 1-2)
   A. Last days (Acts 2:17)
      Isaiah 2:2
   B. All nations (Acts 2:5)
      1) Isaiah 2:2
      2) Luke 24:47
   C. Jerusalem (Acts 2:5)
      1) Isaiah 2:3
      2) Luke 24:44-49
   D. Eternal kingdom (Acts 2:37-42)
      Daniel 2:44, 7:18
   E. Date of coming approximately 33 A.D. (Acts 1-2)
      1) Old testament prophecy
      2) John the Baptist –"is near" Matthew 3:1-2
      3) Jesus—"is near" Matthew 4:17
   F. Lifetime (Acts 1:18-19, 2:14)
      Mark 9:1 "Some"—Judas died
   G. Power (Acts 1:8, Acts 2:1-4)
      Mark 9:1
   H. New birth (Acts 2:38)
      Water and Spirit John 3:1-7
   I. Kingdom within (Acts 2:37)
      Luke 17:20-21
   J. Peter with the keys (Acts 2:14, 38)
      Matthew 16:19
   K. Repentance and forgiveness of sin (Acts 2:38)
      Luke 24:44-49

4. Conclusion
   A. The church is the kingdom of God on earth established in approximately 33 A.D.
   B. Acts 2:42 As citizens of the kingdom and members of the body (the church), we must be devoted to:
      1.) Doctrine
      2.) Fellowship
      3.) Breaking bread
      4.) Prayer
   C. Matthew 6:33 We must seek his kingdom first. Ask them to commit themselves to at least Sunday services and midweek services.

NOTES:

Light and Darkness I

Introduction: 1 Peter 2:9-10

Darkness Not a People of God No Mercy	Light People of God Mercy
Lost Not a Christian Not a Disciple	Saved Christian Disciple

A. Every person is either in the darkness or the light. There is no twilight zone.

B. Where are you?

1. Darkness

A. Isaiah 59:1-2

1) Sin separates us from God.

WALL

DARKNESS MAN		LIGHT GOD

SIN

2) In order for a man to have a relationship with God the wall must be broken down—sin must be forgiven.

3) The point in time sin is forgiven is the point in time a person is saved.

B. Romans 3:23-25

1) Who has sinned? Everyone!

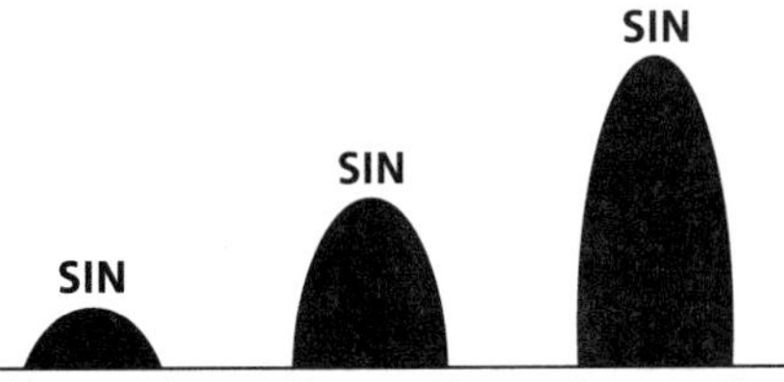

2) Who is further away from God? All equal, all lost. Therefore a good moral life does not save you.

3) Faith in the blood of Jesus saves you (v. 25).

C. What is Sin?

1) Galatians 5:19-21 (sins of commission)

2) James 4:17 (sins of omission)

D. What is the eternal consequence of sin? Romans 6:23

Wages of Sin	Gift of God
Death Hell Darkness	Eternal Life Heaven Light

Just two alternatives

2. Light

A. John 3:1-7

1) Born again (v. 3), born of water and spirit (v. 5), born again (v. 7)

2) Personal decision as an adult

B. What message must one believe to be in the light (to be saved?) Acts 2:22-24.

1) Jesus is from God—miracles (v. 22).

2) Jesus raised physically from the dead (v. 24).

3) Everyone is responsible for the crucifixion of Christ (v. 23). All have sinned (Romans 3:23).

C. Response of people Acts 2:37

1) Cut to the heart

2) What shall we do?

D. Once the people believed, what did they do? Acts 2:38-42

1) Repent (Greek = to turn)

2) Be baptized (Greek = to be immersed).

3) Purpose of Baptism
   a. Sin forgiven—Therefore this is the point in time a person is saved.
   b. Holy Spirit given to each who responded—power to live as God commands

E. Baptism Romans 6:1-4
Baptism is the sharing (a participation) in the death, burial and resurrection of Christ (more than just a symbol).

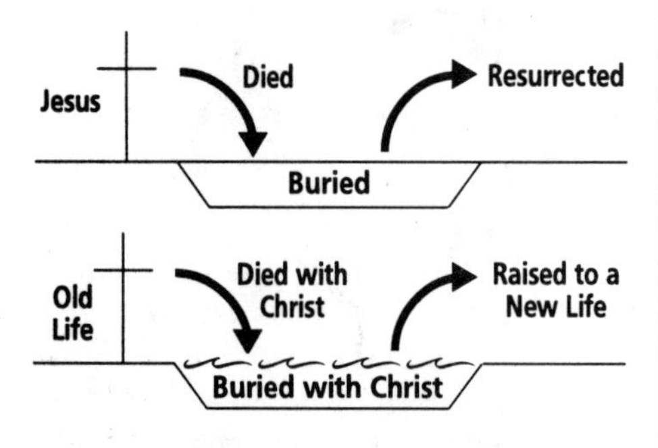

DARKNESS	LIGHT
Sin Separates from God	Acts 2:38 Sin is Forgiven
Born Again of Water and Spirit John 3:5	Acts 2:38 Water = Baptism Spirit = Received at Baptism
Romans 3:25 Faith in the Blood of Jesus Saves Us	Jesus shed his blood when he died. In Baptism we share by faith in the death, burial and resurrection of Jesus. Thus we contact the blood in baptism and are forgiven of our sins and SAVED!

3. Traditions/False Doctrines—Matthew 15:6-9
   A. Infant Baptism
      1) Personal faith is needed (Colossians 2:12).
      2) Began approximately third century A.D.
      3) Original sin
         a. Ezekiel 18:20
         b. Became "church doctrine" in 549 A.D.
   B. Praying Jesus into your heart
      1) Revelation 3:20—taken out of context. This verse is addressed to Christians.
      2) Began in the early 1800s in America.
   C. Bible—True Doctrine
      Hear, Believe, Repent, Confess, Be Baptized

4. Sinful nature
Suggest to the individual with whom you are studying that he or she write a description of their sinful nature, and then be specific about various sins they have committed. This is so that they might see the gravity and magnitude of their sin. He or she should keep this for personal use.

NOTES:

Light and Darkness II

1. Review of Plan of Salvation

A. Hear	Romans 10:17
B. Believe	Hebrews 11:6
C. Repent	Luke 13:3
D. Confess	Romans 10:9, 1 Timothy 6:12
E. Baptized	Acts 2:38, 1 Peter 3:21

2. The Major Conversions in Acts
   A. Conversions

1) Acts 2:36-47	First Christian in Jerusalem
2) Acts 8:26-39	Ethiopian Eunuch
3) Acts 16:22-34	Philippian jailer and his family
4) Acts 18:24-26	Apollos
5) Acts 19:1-5	Ephesians
6) Acts 9:1-22	Paul
7) Acts 22:3-16	Paul

   B. Questions concerning Conversions
      1) What was preached?
      2) What was the person's (people's) response to the message?
      3) How long did the person (people) take to make the decision?
      4) What was their response after baptism?

3. Refuting False Doctrines
   A. *"Pray Jesus into your heart"*: This phrase is never mentioned in the Bible. People may use Revelation 3:20 about Jesus knocking at the door, however, you must examine the Scripture in context. This scripture does not teach how to become a Christian and be saved, but how to come back to God after becoming lukewarm. It is addressed to disciples who already responded to Christ in faith, repentance, confession and baptism.
   B. *"Accept Jesus into your heart"*: (Same teaching as praying Jesus into your heart—just different terminology.) Based on Romans 10:9. You must look at scripture in context. Paul is addressing the problem of the Israelites: unbelief that Jesus was the Christ, the Son of God. Read further on to Romans 10:13. When do you call on the name of the Lord? At baptism (Acts 22:16).
   C. *Infant baptism:* A baby cannot have faith, and since we are baptized through faith in the power of God (Colossians 2:12), babies cannot be baptized.
   D. *Original sin:* Ezekiel 18:20 teaches there is no original sin; each person is responsible for his own actions and will be judged accordingly. Therefore babies are born sinless and will be saved if they die.
   E. *"Baptism does not save you"*: 1 Peter 3:21 says that baptism *does* save you through the resurrection of Jesus Christ. Acts 2:38 teaches that sin is forgiven at baptism—one is saved at the point sin is forgiven.

F. *"Baptism is a work—yet we are saved by faith"* (Ephesians 2:8): Colossians 2:12 teaches we are saved by *faith*—in the working of God at baptism.

G. *"Baptism is an outward sign of an inward grace":* Romans 6:2-4 states that baptism is an actual participation in the death, burial and resurrection of Christ. It is not merely a sign, seal or symbol.

H. *"Baptism isn't important, after all, look at what Paul said about it in 1 Corinthians 1:17"*: Paul does not diminish the importance of baptism here. (Paul himself was baptized to have his sins forgiven in Acts 22:16.) In context (read 1 Corinthians 1:10-17), he makes the point that he does not want people following men (denominationalism). He mentions baptism several times in the passage.

I. *"The thief on the cross was not baptized and Jesus told him that they would see each other in paradise":* Jesus had not even died yet, and baptism is participating in his death (Romans 6:2-4); also on earth, he had the power to forgive sins (Matthew 9:2-6).

J. *"Believer's baptism"*: This is baptism as an adult, but is not done in conjunction with the understanding that one is being saved at this point in time (John 3:5, Acts 2:38). "Retroactive understanding" is not sufficient for salvation.

NOTES:

The Cross

1. Passion Account
   Read Matthew 26:31 - 28:10.
   Suggested Reading Intervals:

26:31-35	27:27-31
26:36-46	27:32-44
26:47-56	27:45-56
26:57-68	27:57-61
26:69-75	27:62-66
27:1-10	28:1-10
27:11-26	

2. Physical Death
   Read the medical account of Jesus' physical death. See page 98.

3. Personal Responsibility
   A. Remember there were many others who died by crucifixion in the first century. It was not that Jesus was painfully crucified that makes him unique—it was that he was crucified for you, in your place. He died on the cross for you.
   B Romans 3:23
   C. Isaiah 59:1-2
   D. Matthew 27:46
   E. Ask the person with whom you are studying to go over their list of sins.
   F. Isaiah 53:4-6 (substitute your name).

NOTES:

Baptism with the Holy Spirit

Introduction: Jesus was given the Spirit in full measure, no limit (John 3:34). There are three measures of the Holy Spirit:

1. The indwelling of the Holy Spirit Received at baptism (Acts 2:38)

2. The baptism with the Holy Spirit
   A. Characteristics in Acts 2 and Acts 10
      1) Promise (not command), Acts 1:4-5
      2) Predicted (prophesied)
      3) Came without warning (People were not specifically praying for it.)
      4) Languages
      5) Purpose: to usher in the Kingdom with power
   B. Accounts of the baptism with the Holy Spirit
      1) To the Jews—in Jerusalem (Acts 2)
      2) To the Gentiles—begins with Cornelius (Acts 10)
         a) Note: Cornelius and his household were water baptized in v. 48, saved at baptism.
         b) Peter explained actions to the Jews (Acts 11:1-18).
         c) "At the beginning," (Acts 11:15)
   C. Does the baptism with the Holy Spirit still exist today?
      Ephesians 4:4-6: There is *one* baptism—which one? (Written about 60-62 A.D.) There are three options:
      1) John's baptism—passed when new covenant began (Acts 19:1-5)
      2) The baptism with the Holy Spirit (Acts 2 and 10). No longer present as it was a prophecy/promise that has been fulfilled. It was never a general command for all Christians.
      3) Baptism with water in the name of Jesus Christ for the forgiveness of sins to receive the indwelling of the Holy Spirit.
         a) Jesus commanded this baptism (Matthew 28:18-20).
         b) This baptism is recorded all the way through the book of Acts and the epistles. 1 Peter 3:21 (also written around 62 a.d.) makes reference to this water baptism of salvation.
         c) It had to be the one baptism of Ephesians 4:4-6 as it was the only one practiced by 60-62 A.D. when Ephesians was written.

3. The miraculous gifts of the Holy Spirit (next lesson).
   A. Received by the apostles' laying on of hands
   B. No longer present today

Miraculous Gifts of the Holy Spirit

1. Types of Miraculous Gifts
   A. 1 Corinthians 12:8-10
      1) Wisdom
      2) Knowledge
      3) Faith
      4) Healing
      5) Miracles
      6) Prophecy
      7) Distinguishing spirits
      8) Tongues
      9) Interpretation
   B. (Mark 16:16-18) Some will be able to:
      1) Drink poison and not die
      2) Be bitten by snakes and not die (Acts 28:5)

2. Types of "Laying on of Hands":
   A. Blessing (Acts 13:3)
   B. Healing
      1) Ananias heals Paul's blindness (Acts 9:17-18)
      2) Paul heals Publius' father on Malta (Acts 28:8)
   C. Passing on the Gifts
      1) Apostles would pass on the gifts (Acts 8:18).
      2) These people could not pass on the gifts they received.
         a) Acts 6:1-8: Context is the choosing of "The Seven." This is the first occasion that the gifts were passed. Stephen immediately starts to perform miraculous signs among the people with God's power (v. 8).
         b) Acts 8:1-25: Context is after Stephen's martyrdom. Great persecution breaks out. Many leave, but apostles stay in Jerusalem. Philip, one of the seven who had received the gifts in Acts 6:1-8, goes to Samaria. He performs many miraculous signs and healings to get people to believe (v. 12), including Simon the Sorcerer (v. 13) and they are baptized. (They became Christians and thus receive the forgiveness of sins and the gift (indwelling) of the Holy Spirit, Acts 2:38.) When apostles came to Samaria, Simon saw the Spirit's gifts were only given by apostles' laying on of hands and offers them money for the ability (Acts 8:18). Note: Simon didn't ask Philip for the gifts because Philip could not pass them on. Simon is rebuked for having the wrong motivation.
         c) Acts 19:1-6: Paul finds disciples in Ephesus who didn't know what the Holy Spirit was because they had only received John's baptism of repentance. Then they were baptized into the name of Jesus Christ to receive the forgiveness of their sins and the indwelling of the Holy Spirit (v.5). Then they received the miraculous gifts of prophecy and speaking in tongues by the laying on of Paul's hands (v.6). Paul was an apostle.

3. General Observations

A. Apostles were able to pass on the gifts because they were apostles. The apostles possessed the ability to perform miracles even during the ministry of Christ (Luke 9:1). This ability to pass and perform the gifts was not given at Pentecost.

B. 1 Corinthians 12 and 14 are not the directives on how to receive tongues (the church there had already received them), but rather the correctives on how to use them because everyone was speaking at the same time and misusing the tongues. 1 Corinthians 12:28-30 shows that tongues as a gift were not given to everyone in the church. Thus the concept of a "Pentecostal church" (every member speaking in tongues) is against scripture.

C. 1 Corinthians 13:8-10 "Perfection" here could not mean the coming of Christ because it is in the neuter gender in Greek, not the masculine gender. When perfection comes probably refers to the canonization of the Bible sometime after the first century. At that time, all the miraculous gifts would be gone because all the apostles and those to whom they passed the gifts would have died.

D. The purpose of the miraculous gifts from 1 Corinthians 14:20-22:
   1) To get non-believers to believe (tongues were only to be used to bring non-believers to faith).
   2) To edify the Christians and strengthen their faith.
   3) Now the Bible fulfills these needs—thus the church today does not need apostles or miraculous gifts.

E. 2 Thessalonians 2:9-10 shows there can be miracles by Satan today. Satan's purpose is to deceive people about the truth, so they will not be saved.

F. Speaking in "tongues" is common in many religions (Mormon, Catholic, Islam, etc.) because religion gets dried and staid. These are also called "ecstatic utterances"—non-understandable sounds and fragments of speech.

G. A person can be filled with the Spirit without speaking in tongues (Ephesians 5:18-19).

H. Jesus never spoke in tongues and he was accorded the full measure of the Spirit (John 3:34-36).

NOTES:

The Church

1. Colossians 1:15-18

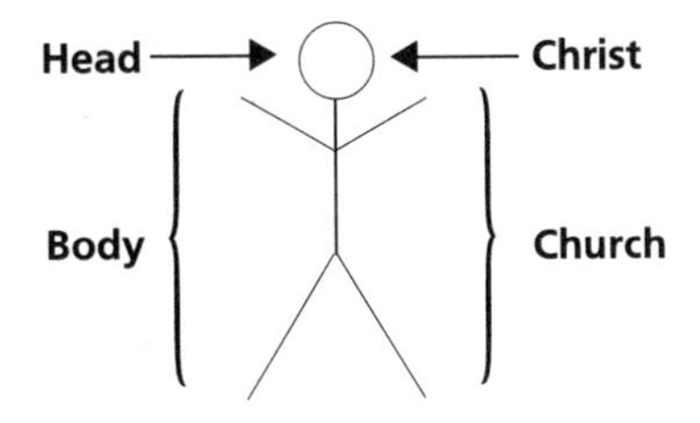

The church is the body of Christ. The body needs the head. The church is essential to Christianity.

2. Ephesians 2:19-21
   A. The church is the family of God.

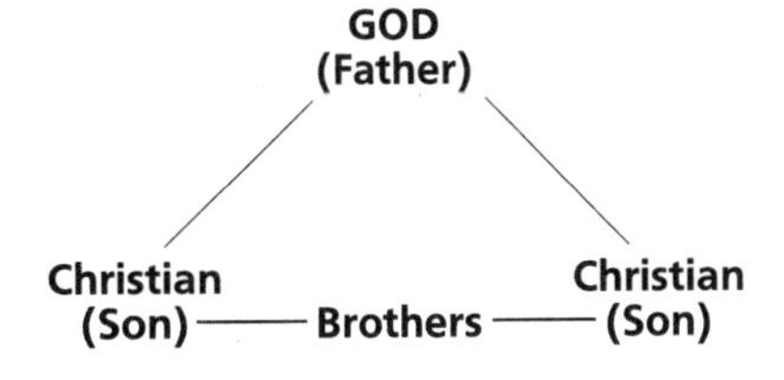

   B. 1 Corinthians 12:12-13: baptized into the body of Christ, the church
   C. Romans 6:3-4 teaches we are also baptized into Christ. Baptism is when we become a Christian, a son of God, and at that same point we become members of the church, the family of God.

3. Ephesians 2:20
   A. Cornerstone: Christ
   B. Foundation: Apostles and Prophets
      1) Apostles = New Testament
      2) Prophets = Old Testament
   C. The church is based on the word of God only.

4. Have you ever wondered why there are so many denominations? (450 or more exist in the U.S. alone.)
   A. The Bible teaches there is one church.
      1) Ephesians 4:4-6—One Body
      2) Romans 12:4-5—One Body
      3) 1 Corinthians 12:12-13—One Body

   B. 1 Corinthians 1:10-13: no divisions. Following personalities and in time their writings (traditions) have caused the divisions (Matthew 15:6-9).
      1) Denominations

de	nomin	ation
Latin	Latin	English
of	name	group

      2) Denomination = a group of a name. Unscriptural according to 1 Corinthians 1:10-13.
      3) Examples:

Lutheran	From Martin Luther
Methodist	From John and Charles Wesley
Presbyterian	From John Calvin and John Knox
Mormon	From Joseph Smith
Catholic	Tradition through the ages

5. What is the one church called in the Bible?
   A. Matthew 16:18: I will build my church.
   B. Romans 16:16: Churches of Christ.
   C. There are other names in the Bible.

6. 1 Corinthians 12:14-27
   A. We need the body. The body needs us (v. 21).
   B. Be involved on a relationship level in the church (v. 26).

7. Hebrews 10:23-25
   A. Do not miss church.
   B. The fellowship helps us to be unswerving in our commitment (v. 23).
   C. Another purpose of fellowship is to encourage each other so we will remain faithful (v. 24).
   D. Must come to all meetings of the body: i.e. Sunday and midweek services, special devotionals, Bible jubilees, retreats, seminars, etc.

NOTES:

FOLLOW-UP STUDY 1

After Baptism, Now What?

(First discipleship partner time)

Introduction

- A. Discuss: first few days as a Christian.
- B. Pray

1. The Conversion of the 3000
   - A. Acts 2:36-47
     - 1) Review how to become a Christian.
     - 2) Reinforce the joy of salvation.
   - B. Devoted—Apostles' Teaching—the Word
     - 1) Assign daily readings, suggesting a chapter a day. Suggested readings:
       - a) Colossians 3
       - b) 1 John 1-5
       - c) 1 Peter 1-5
     - 2) Show how to mark Bible. For many a quiet time book is helpful.
   - C. Fellowship
     - 1) Discuss the purpose of each gathering: Sunday and midweek services, devotionals, discipleship partner times.
     - 2) Discuss the expectation to tithe (10%). Read together Malachi 3:6-12.
   - D. Prayer
     - 1) Discuss faith (Mark 11:22-24).
     - 2) Share answered prayers.
   - E. Breaking Bread—Communion (1 Corinthians 11:23-32)
     - 1) Discuss purpose of bread and fruit of the vine.
     - 2) Prevents a hardness of heart

2. The Conversion of Paul (Acts 9:18-25)
   - A. Paul immediately begins to preach.
     - 1) Who have you shared with?
     - 2) List people to share with.
   - B. Paul grows powerful.
   - C. Paul is persecuted.

Conclusion

Pray together (suggest on knees).

FOLLOW-UP STUDY 2

Christ Is Your Life

(Second discipleship partner time)

Introduction

A. Discuss:

1) Did you have daily quiet times this past week?

2) Who did you share with and invite?

3) Did you feel good about your level of sacrifice in time and money?

B. Pray

1. Colossians 3:1-4

A. Raised with Christ in baptism (Colossians 2:12)

B. Set your mind (thoughts) and set your heart (emotions) on things above.

C. Christ is your life.

2. Put to death (Colossians 3:5-11)

A. Be open about your greatest struggles this week.

B. Discuss practical ways to crucify these sins.

3. Put on (Colossians 3:12-14)

A. Compassion

B. Kindness

C. Humility

D. Gentleness

E. Patience

4. New attitudes (Colossians 3:5-11)

A. Peace (v. 15)

B. Thankful (vv. 15-16)

C. Wholehearted (v. 17)

D. Family interaction (v. 18-21)

E. Employer—employee relationship (3:22, 4:1)

F. Teacher—student relationship

Conclusion

Pray together (suggest on knees).

FOLLOW-UP STUDY 3

Best Friends of All Time

(Third discipleship partner time)

Introduction

A. Discuss:
   1) Your relationship with God
   2) What are you reading?
   3) Who are you sharing with?

B. Pray.

1. One Another Passages:
   A. Love one another (John 13:34-35). Jesus teaches that Christians should have better relationships than people in the world. Set your mind to make the Christians around you your best friends.
   B. Counsel one another (Colossians 1:28-29). God's plan for maturity
   C. Restore one another, bear burdens (Galatians 6:1-2). Handling pressure— discuss openness
   D. Confess sins to one another (James 5:16).
   E. Attitudes towards one another (1 Thessalonians 5:12-14)
   F. Discuss how to have daily contact with one another (Hebrews 3:12-14).
   G. Prevent "bad attitudes" in one another (Hebrews 12:15).
   H. Confront one another (Matthew 18:15-17). Church discipline begins one-on-one and rarely should go to steps 2, 3 and 4.
   I. Pray for one another—it makes a difference (Ephesians 6:18).
   J. The ultimate goal of love and unity—world evangelism (John 17:20-23)

2. For further private study:

Matthew 22:37-39	Philippians 2:1-5
Romans 12:4-8	Philippians 3:17
Romans 12-9-16	1 Thessalonians 2:8
Romans 13:7	1 Thessalonians 2:19-20
Romans 14:1	1 Thessalonians 5:11
Romans 15:14	Titus 3:1-9
Ephesians 4:25-32	Hebrews 10:24-25
Ephesians 5:19	James 2:15-16

Conclusion

Pray together (suggest on knees).

FOLLOW-UP STUDY 4
The Mission

(Fourth discipleship-partner time)

Introduction

- A. Discuss:
  - 1) How are you feeling about your discipling relationship?
  - 2) How are you feeling about your relationship with God?
- B. Pray.

1. Jesus' Mission
   - A. Luke 19:10
   - B. 1 Timothy 1:15
   - C. Acts 20:24
   - D. Matthew 28:19-20
     - 1) What was Jesus' mission?
     - 2) What is our mission?

2. Disciples must go...
   - A. John 15:1-16
     - 1) Relationship with God
     - 2) Jesus' plan to multiply
   - B. See the growth of the church when all Christians are fruitful (making disciples).
     - 1) Acts 2:41
     - 2) Acts 2:47
     - 3) Acts 4:4
     - 4) Acts 5:14
     - 5) Acts 6:1
     - 6) Acts 6:7
     - 7) Acts 8:4
   - C. Discuss:
     - 1) World Evangelism
     - 2) Mission Teams
     - 3) Your Dreams

3. Persecution will come...
   - A. John 15:18-16:4. Jesus was called these names, lies and half-truths.
     - 1) Matthew 11:19
     - 2) Mark 3:21 (by his family)
     - 3) Mark 3:22
     - 4) Luke 23:2
     - 5) John 8:48
     - 6) John 9:16
   - B. Attitude of Jesus
     - 1) Luke 23:24
     - 2) Hebrews 12:1-2
   - C. Attitude of Apostles
     Acts 5:40-42

Conclusion

Pray together (suggest on knees).

Additional Studies for Making Disciples

Originally printed under the title, *Making Disciples,* edited by Randy McKean.

Studies on "God's Wisdom vs. Man's Wisdom" and "The Grace of God" by Thomas A. Jones.

Setting Up the Study

1. Approach to setting up a study:
   A. Set up a time to talk. Make sure the atmosphere of the meeting place is conducive to good conversation. Have the gift Bible ready to present to them if they choose to study.
   B. Share about yourself. Tell them about your conversion, what you were generally like before you became a Christian, and why you became a Christian.
   C. Ask them where they think they are spiritually. Ask them what some of the most important times in shaping their ideas and beliefs about God and religion were. Work questions like the following into the conversation:
      - Do you believe in the God of the Bible?
      - Do you believe that Jesus is the Son of God? God in the flesh?
      - Do you believe God raised Jesus from the dead?
      - Do you believe the Bible is the word of God? And that we will be judged by it?
      - Have you read the Bible? How much? When?
      - Do you consider yourself a Christian?
      - Do you believe in heaven and hell?
      - Do you believe you would go to heaven if you died right now?
      - Do you want to become a Christian?
   D. Read Matthew 7:7-8.
      1) These are promises with conditions.
      2) Every person must take initiative and put forth effort. God guarantees these promises:
         a) Ask—given to you
         b) Seek—will find
         c) Knock—door will be opened.
      3) To find God, to learn the truth, to get answers, and to learn what life is all about, effort is needed. Examples: Learning a sport, the piano, a language, etc.
      4) It will take time. It will be worth it. I look forward to our friendship deepening as we share our lives and explore the Scriptures together.
      5) It will take an attitude of "teach me; I want to learn."
   E. Invitation
      1) I would like to study the Bible with you as often as possible.
      2) Studying will help you make a decision about following Jesus.
      3) Let me explain the studies to you in general. (Do a verbal overview of the First Principles study series and explain specifically the topics you will study together: discipleship, sin, repentance, cross, baptism.
      4) Let's set a time for the first study.

2. Helpful notes about studying the Bible:
   A. Buy the friend with whom you are studying a Bible as a gift.
   B. Build a good friendship, and help the person with whom you are studying to have other great friends in the church. Have a Christian friend or two join in on the studies.
   C. Take concise notes for your non-Christian friend, so they can go back and review what they have learned. Or come prepared with notes for the study that you can give to them afterwards.
   D. Be sure that you move their heart and not just transfer information with each study. The individual must make his or her own decisions about what was studied; you must specifically call for these. Before moving to the next study, a heart-to-heart talk may be necessary.
   E. Close out the studies with a short prayer. When the person studying feels comfortable with it, have them say a short prayer also.
   F. For those who do not believe in Jesus use one of two approaches: 1) Study through the gospel of John, or 2) study through the Jesus studies.
   G. Use the follow-up studies (at least one per week) with new Christians.

Seeking God

Introduction: What are you looking for in life?

1. Acts 17:16-21
   Briefly explain the situation in Athens.

2. Acts 17:22-28
   A. Why did God create you and bring you to this very place and time? So that you would seek him in order to have a personal relationship with him.
   B. Why do so few people seek God today?
      1) Not only is God unknown (v.23), but the image of God is perverted. We wouldn't want a god like that.
      2) We've created our own gods. We all worship something.
      3) We need to change our idea of God, i.e. powerful, personal, etc. (vv. 24-26).
      4) There's nothing comparable to or more important than knowing our Creator, God.

3. Jeremiah 29:11-14
   A. Have you ever done anything with all of your heart? What was it?
   B. We will find God if we seek him with all of our hearts.

4. Examples of people who sought God:
   A. Acts 8:26-40
      1) Important man; very busy
      2) Still finds time for God (Jerusalem trip).
      3) Takes initiative to read the Scriptures on his own.
      4) Humble; asks for help.
      5) Makes a decision about the things he learned.
      6) Acts on his decision.
      7) Rejoices because he has come to know God.
   B. Acts 17:11-12
      1) Noble character; integrity
      2) Enthusiastic
      3) Daily examined the Scriptures; it was their personal search.
      4) Even though Paul was a respected church leader, they still wanted to look up what he said for themselves. They wanted to have their own convictions.
   C. John 1:18
      1) Where to begin in knowing God?
      2) Jesus has made God known.
      3) To the degree you know Jesus, to that same degree you will know God.

D. John 20:30-31
   1) By believing in Jesus, you will have true life now and eternal life later.
   2) John was an eyewitness to Jesus' life and ministry.
   3) There is power in the word of God to create faith. For example, an acorn has power placed in it to produce a giant oak.

5. Decisions/Reminders/Commitments
   A. Keep reading the Bible.
   B. Let's set up a time and date for our next study before we go.
   C. Always remember we are moving toward the decision that Jesus is the Son of God and the decision to follow Jesus!
   D. Review the Scriptures we have looked at on your own.

NOTES:

Evidences for Jesus

1. Matthew 16:13
   A. Who do you personally say Jesus is?
   B. Jesus claimed to be the Son of God (John 5:24; 8:23-24; 10:30; 14:6-7).
   C. What are the possibilities? Was that claim true or false?
      1) If false, then Jesus either:
         a) Was a mythical character that didn't exist: *Legend.*
         b) Knew that his claims were false: *Liar.*
         c) Didn't know his claims were false: *Lunatic.*
      2) If true, then Jesus is Lord.
      3) Comments:
         a) Extra-biblical manuscripts prove Jesus to be a historical figure, therefore he was not a legend.
         b) Jesus' teachings and the impact of his life make it impossible to entertain the possibility that Jesus was either a liar or lunatic. Would the greatest ethical teachings in the world have come from a liar or from a lunatic?
         c) We must not conclude that Jesus was simply a good moral teacher. That option is not open to us, because it would mean that Jesus lied when he claimed to be the son of God.
         d) There is strong evidence to support the fact that Jesus is clearly Lord, the Son of God as he claimed. Let's look at the evidence.

2. Evidences
   A. Miracles: Attested to by numerous eyewitnesses (John 20:30-31).
   B. Prophecies fulfilled:
      1) Born of a virgin: Isaiah 7:14; Matthew 1:18, 24, 25
      2) House of David: Jeremiah 23:5; Luke 3:23, 31
      3) Born in Bethlehem: Micah 5:2; Matthew 2:1
      4) Ministry to begin in Galilee: Isaiah 9:1; Matthew 4:12-13, 17
      5) Betrayed by a friend: Psalm 41:9; Matthew 10:4; Matthew 26:49-50
      6) Sold for 30 pieces of silver: Zechariah 11:12; Matthew 26:15
      7) Wounded and bruised: Isaiah 53:5; Matthew 27:26
      8) Bones not broken: Psalm 34:20; John 19:32-33
      9) Crucified with thieves: Isaiah 53:12; Matthew 27:38
      10) Resurrection: Psalm 16:10; Acts 2:31
      11) There are more than 400 Messianic prophecies. Jesus fulfills them all! The probability that any man might have lived and fulfilled just 8 prophecies is 1 in 10 to the 17th power or 1 in 100,000,000,000,000,000.

C. Jesus' life and teaching: His teachings surpass human wisdom while his life exemplifies them perfectly (John 7:17).

D. The Resurrection: This is perhaps the most convincing of all the evidences. Was Jesus raised from the dead? The response is critically important. Read 1 Corinthians 15:12-19.

   1) The Prediction: Matthew 27:62-66. Jesus' predictions about his own resurrection were so well known that guards were posted at the tomb. This raised the question: Did he really die? Perhaps he passed out on the cross and was later revived.

   2) The Death: John 19:31-34. Professional executioners would not make such a basic error as to think a live person was dead. Medical experts indicate that the water that flowed from Jesus' pierced side would be from the pericardium, a sac around the heart that fills with water when the heart ruptures. Jesus was clearly dead. But perhaps they visited the wrong tomb and mistakenly thought he was raised.

   3) The Wrong Tomb
      a) The tomb was near the cross: John 19:38-42.
      b) Mary saw where he was buried. Pilate knew where to send the guards: Matthew 27:61-66. They didn't visit the wrong tomb. So let's visit the tomb.

   4) The Empty Tomb: Matthew 28:11-15. Was the tomb empty? If not, the Jews would have produced the body. The fact that they tried to explain away the empty tomb shows that it was empty. So, was the body stolen as they claimed?

   5) The Stolen Body: It would have been incredibly difficult for anyone to steal the body considering the huge stone and the Roman guards in front of the tomb. In any case, there are two possibilities: Someone other than the disciples stole the body; therefore, the disciples were deceived and wistfully hallucinated the risen Christ or the disciples stole the body and hoaxed the resurrection. Let's consider the first possibility:
      a) Someone other than the disciples stole the body. John 20:19-29. Disciples are scared and hiding, having earlier fled at Jesus' arrest. Was this a mass hallucination? Thomas, the skeptic, touched Jesus. This was no hallucination to Thomas. But perhaps the resurrection was all a hoax, the second possibility...
      b) The disciples stole the body. Acts 4:12-13. Remember the cowardly disciples? (Matthew 26:56). Peter who denied Jesus? They are now men

of remarkable courage. Yet, something has happened. In fact, according to early church history, each of the disciples died a martyr's death, except John:

- Peter—crucified head downward
- Thomas—speared to death
- James—beheaded by Herod (Acts 12:1-2)
- Matthew—martyred
- Andrew—crucified
- James—crucified
- Philip—martyred
- Jude—shot with arrows
- Simon the Zealot—crucified
- Bartholomew—flogged to death
- Matthias—axed to death

Why did these men endure such atrocities? Who would suffer and die for a lie that gains them nothing? When men are all alone and under pressure, they crack. These men did not. Why not?

6) These men had seen Jesus raised from the dead: 1 Corinthians 15:1-6. In fact, over 500 people at once saw the resurrected Jesus. Indeed, Jesus has been raised. The proof is logical and overwhelming.

3. Conclusion: Christianity is true and reasonable: Acts 26:24-29. Jesus is the Son of God! Now what remains is to make the decision to follow him.

NOTES:

Note: *True and Reasonable* by Douglas Jacoby is an excellent book for evidences and is available from Discipleship Publications International.

Who Is Jesus Christ?

1. John 1:1, 14
   A. Jesus is God in the flesh.
   B. Imagine you are all-powerful, and you want to communicate with an ant colony to let them understand how much you love them. How would you do it without terrifying them? Become an ant yourself.

2. Colossians 2:9
   A. All of the fullness of God lives in Christ. This means that every aspect of God's character can be seen in Christ. Let's look at Jesus' character...
   B. Mark 4:35-41
   Jesus, like God, is all-powerful, controlling nature. Jesus is fully God.
   C. Luke 4:1-13
   Yet Jesus, like man, was tempted by selfishness (v.3), materialism and power (vv.6-7), and pride (vv.-10). He used the Scriptures to fight temptation, and so he was without sin (2 Corinthians 5:21).
   D. Hebrews 2:14-18
   Jesus shared in our humanity so he could free us from fear and help us when we are tempted.
   E. Hebrews 4:14-16
   Jesus, like God, can sympathize with our weaknesses. He can relate to us.
   F. Mark 1:29-39
   Jesus compassionately met people's needs (vv. 29-33). Prayer was a top priority for him (v.35). He was intent on his purpose (v.38).
   G. Luke 23:32-43
   Jesus, like God, is forgiving and filled with love.

3. 1 John 2:3-6 The goal of the Christian is to live like Jesus. This must be our purpose if we are to be Christians.

4. John 14:6
   A. The Way—exclusive, not just a way, but the *only* way to God.
   B. The Truth—not just some truth, but the *whole* truth of God.
   C. The Life—not another alternative, but *the* life we were created to live: an attractive, successful and fulfilling life!
   D. Acts 4:12: This decision is the most important decision of your life.

Man's Wisdom vs. God's Wisdom

1. Everyone on earth is asking the question in one form or another: *How Can I Really Live?*

2. The Bible says there are two ways to answer that:

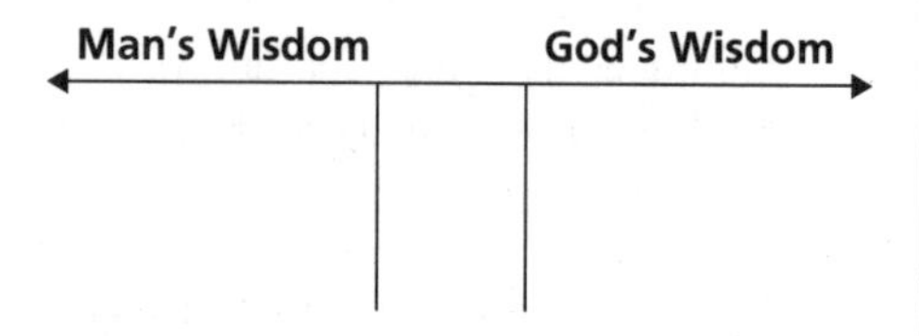

1 Corinthians 1:18-20

A. Where does the cross belong? Wisdom of man or wisdom of God?

B. How does man, in his wisdom, view the cross?

C. How does God, in his wisdom, view all of man's wisdom?

D. If I think you are a fool and you think I am a fool, what will be true about our relationship?

E. What is the relationship then between the wisdom of man and the wisdom of God? We are dealing with two things going in opposite directions, two things totally opposed to one another. (See James 4:4.)

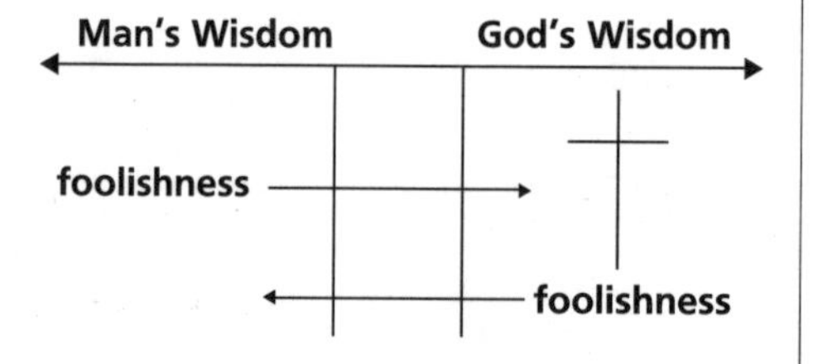

1 Corinthians 3:18-20

F. What does "he must become a 'fool,' and he can become wise" mean?

G. Again, what is the strong message? God's wisdom and man's are total opposites.

H. You cannot straddle the fence. The gulf is too wide.

Matthew 16:13-23

I. What does "Peter rebuked Jesus" mean?

J. What was Jesus' response?

K. Where does "man's wisdom" really come from? Satan. Jesus is clear. No wonder it is the opposite of God's wisdom.

L. *Important question: What is man's wisdom about "how to really live?"* What do you learn from television, from the streets, from movies, from the talk shows? What is the world telling us we must do to really find life? "Look out for number one." "Get what you want." "Get the power, the pleasure, the control you want." "Get the money." "Protect yourself." "Guard your rights." "Maintain your independence." "Get a good lawyer." Etc.

What then is at the center of man's wisdom?

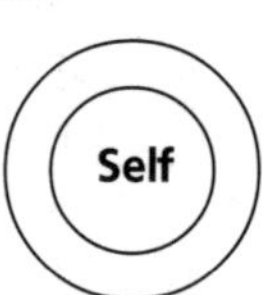

3. Matthew 16:24-26
What is Jesus' message? What is his wisdom about how to really live? Just the opposite of the world's message. Definitely a radical message.
   A. Deny self? What does this mean?
      1) *Arneomai* in Greek means to disown. A strong word. What does it mean if you disown your son or daughter? How much support? How many letters? The word here is an unusually strong form of this verb. *Aparneomai*. The "*ap*" prefix means utterly.
      2) Jesus is saying we have all lived on man's side. We have all put self at the center. Now we need to totally disown that old person and turn to an opposite way of living.
   B. "Take up the cross." What does this mean? What were crosses for? Death. Put to death the old life. Don't defend it. Don't support it. Put it to death.
   C. "Follow me." Why is it impossible to do this without doing the things mentioned above? Note: It is impossible to follow Jesus without meeting his conditions of discipleship.
   D. What does Jesus say the bottom line will be for people who live on man's side? He who "saves" his life (guards it and protects it) will lose it.
   E. What is the bottom line for those foolish people who "lose their lives for his sake?" They will find their lives. They will really live. Jesus' own life, death and resurrection is proof of what he taught.

This is how to find life.

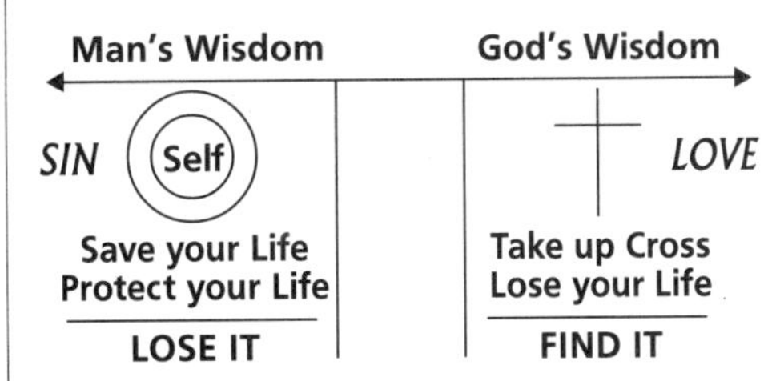

4. Additional thoughts
   A. What is everything on the left side of the diagram called? Sin.
   B. What is everything on the right side called? Love. Love for God and love for others. Living for God and living for others.
   C. How have you lived according to man's wisdom? What are your greatest tendencies in this direction?
   D. When did you make the decision to renounce man's wisdom and commit yourself to following God's plan?
   E. Which side was Peter on? Which side would Jesus say you are on? Which do you want to be on?

5. Later, you can look at the following diagram and show that repentance and baptism bring forgiveness of all of man's sin (left side of the diagram) and power through the Holy Spirit to live out God's plan (right side of the diagram).

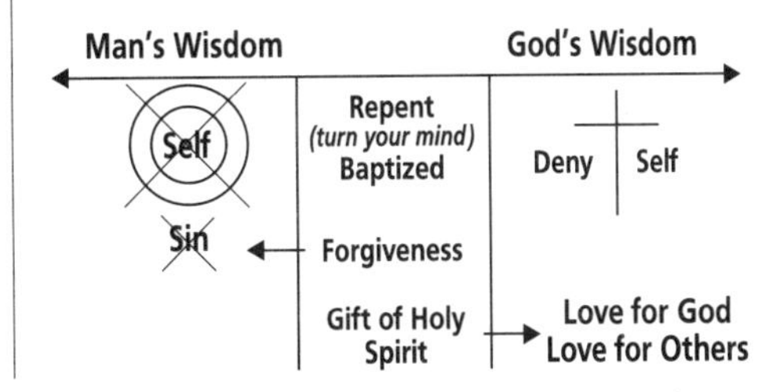

The Grace of God

1. 2 Corinthians 5:10—Do you feel confident about standing before the judgment seat of Christ? Why or why not? In this study we will learn how we can be completely confident about standing before God.

2. There are over 110 specific references to the grace of God in the New Testament and many other times when the concept is alluded to. Grace is a major biblical theme.
   A. Acts 14:26—What does "the grace of God" mean to you?
   B. Acts 20:24—Why was the message of Jesus called "the gospel of God's grace?"

3. There are two basic ways that people could be saved (be accepted by God):
   A. *Works model*—Earning our place with God by doing all the right things.
      1) Here the standard is perfection.
         a) James 2:10—To even fail at one point is to be guilty of all. One sin would keep one from being saved by works.
         b) Galatians 5:3—Written to those taking *certain* works and making them the standard for salvation.
         c) Romans 3:23—Based on the works model everyone falls short, and no one will be right with God.
      2) If God made anything less than perfection acceptable, where do you think he should draw the line? 95? 90? 80? 65? How fair would God be to save the person who made a 65 on the morality scale and condemn the person just a point behind at 64? God can have only one performance standard—perfection!
   B. *Grace model*—God giving us salvation as a gift that we have not earned and do not deserve.
      1) Here your perfection or performance is not the issue. The issue is what Christ has done.
         a) Romans 3:22-25a—"Justified" (declared not guilty) freely by his grace
         b) Romans 4:4-8—Why is the person who comes to Christ totally saved? (Because the righteousness of Christ is "credited" to his or her account.)
         c) Colossians 1:21-23—How does God view a person who has been reconciled to him through Christ? Holy, without blemish and free from accusation! Is such a one really without blemish? Why does God view him or her this way?
      2) This grace was made available only because Jesus was willing to pay the enormous price that had to be paid for sin.

a) 2 Corinthians 8:9—He became poor for our sakes.
b) Hebrews 2:9—He experienced death for all men.
c) 1 Peter 1:18-19—We are redeemed, not with perishable things, but with the precious blood of Christ.
d) 1 John 5:8-10—What does all this mean? God loves us! He loved us so much he sent Jesus to die for our sins so we might be saved by grace!

4. If salvation is not by works but by grace, is everyone saved?
   A. Hebrews 2:9—Who did Jesus die for?
   B. 1 Timothy 2:3-5—How many does God want saved?
   C. 2 Thessalonians 1:6-10—Are all people going to be saved? If Jesus died for all and wants to give grace to all but not all are going to be saved, what does that tell us? We must accept his offer. We must receive the pardon. We must say "Yes, I want the relationship with God that comes by grace."
   Illustration: A pardon that is not accepted does not become a pardon.
   D. Acts 2:36-39
   How did Peter tell his listeners to accept the grace of God?
      1) Repentance—turning to Christ and away from the world.
      2) Baptism—giving God your old life to bury, so by grace he can raise up a new life.
      What gifts did he promise that God would freely give?
      3) Forgiveness of sins—because we have trusted in what Jesus did.
      4) The Holy Spirit—to help us live the new life.

5. Who can be *completely confident* about his or her salvation?
   A. The person who has accepted God's grace just as these people did in Acts 2.
   B. The person who keeps his or her faith in Jesus and never leaves him. Colossians 1:22-23; Hebrews 3:14 Confidence rests on what Jesus has done. If we are responding in faith to him, it is his work that saves us—not our own performance. Our performance will vary. His work of salvation never does. He redeems us. He justifies us. He reconciles us. We are secure.

6. What is the only right response to "salvation by grace?"
   A. 1 John 3:1—Rejoicing and amazement
   B. 1 Corinthians 15:9-10—Total commitment to Jesus

7. Have you accepted God's grace? Are you saved by his grace?

Repentance

(To be done in connection with the Light and Darkness studies)

1. Who needs repentance?
   A. Luke 13:1-5
      1) Everyone must repent.
      2) There are no degrees of sinners.
      3) Alternative to repentance is perishing.
   B. Acts 26:20-21
      1) Repentance=change of heart/mind. It is a decision.
      2) Repentance literally means "to turn around." (Go a different direction.)
      3) Repentance is a *positive* command—change to become what we were created to be—like Jesus!
      4) Repentance is followed by deeds—your life reflects the change.
      5) Can be done in an instant, though effects last a lifetime.
      6) Preaching the biblical message of repentance leads to opposition. (Some do not want to change. Many do not appreciate being told the truth about their life.)
2. 2 Corinthians 7:8-11
   A. Worldly sorrow and godly sorrow. Examples:
      Speeding: The officer pulls you over. Worldly sorrow. You're sorry you got caught. Good chance you will speed again. Godly sorrow: You're sorry that you have broken the law, endangered lives, etc. In both cases you are sorry, but repentance (change in lifestyle) comes only with godly sorrow.
      Pregnancy: Your girlfriend gets pregnant. Worldly sorrow: Sorry about the consequences. Start to use contraceptives. May have an abortion. Godly sorrow: Will never be immoral again.
   B. Godly sorrow produces a visible change in one's character and lifestyle. Therefore you can tell whether or not someone has repented.
   C. 1 Peter 2:22-25
      1) Godly sorrow—understands that our sin hurts God (put Jesus on the cross).
      2) If in love with God—will not want to hurt him—will not want to sin (sin/dog analogy).
      3) Returning to let God direct our lives—that's repentance.

D. Mark 9:42-48
   1) Radical attitude toward sin
   2) World's attitude: Sin is okay in moderation.
   3) God's attitude: Sin is always wrong—deal with sin radically.

E. Acts 3:19-20
   1) Once we repent, there will be times of refreshing.
   2) Must repent in order to have sins forgiven.

Conclusion

A. Do you think you have repented in accordance with what the Bible teaches?
B. How many people do you think have truly repented?
C. What do you need to repent of? Suggest to the individual you are studying with to write out a list of their sins so they can see the gravity and magnitude of sin.
D. Do you really want to repent?

NOTES:

Lordship

Introduction

This study is to help make sure that all of your friend's "life issues" are dealt with before counting the cost. Each person has different main life issues, so spend more time on the ones which are more challenging.

1. Concept of Lordship
   A. 1 Corinthians 1:2-9
      1) "Lord" is used six times in eight verses. There is an obvious emphasis on this concept.
      2) Jesus was known as "Lord" in the Bible.
      3) Definition of "Lord": ruler, master, controller, priority.
      4) Making Jesus "Lord" is giving your life over to his control.
      5) But remember that he is a loving, caring, gracious and forgiving ruler/master.
   B. 2 Peter 3:18
      1) "Lord" and "Savior" are eternally connected in the mind of God.
      2) Jesus is either Lord of all or not your savior at all.
      3) To be saved, you must have Jesus as your Lord in all areas of your life.

2. Implications of Jesus Being Lord
   A. Lord of our conduct
      1) You must repent of all your sin for all time.
      2) Repent of sins including smoking, sexual immorality, drunkenness, grudges, cheating, hatred, prejudice, overeating, etc.
      3) What will be the most difficult sin for you to change or give up or deal with?
   B. Lord of our time
      1) You need to attend all church services or you won't develop well spiritually (Hebrews 10:25; Matthew 6:33). Explain meetings of the body and their purposes fully: Sunday services, midweek services, discipleship groups, devotionals, Bible Jubilees, Bible Talks, retreats, seminars, conferences.
      2) Evangelism is your new purpose with the focus of bringing people to hear the Word preached and explained.
      3) Your daily time with God in prayer and Bible study must be consistent (quiet times).
      4) It is important to have a kingdom perspective when it comes to recreation and vacations.
   C. Lord and Savior of only the biblically saved
      1) Every disciple must have deep conviction about who is lost and who is saved.
      2) You are still lost.
      3) Others like you are lost: family, friends, old church friends, etc. How do you feel about this? How can you help them?
   D. Lord of the one true church
      1) Ephesians 4:4: Only those who are scriptural Christians are members of the one true church.

2) No church can be the true church if it is not baptizing those ready to be disciples for forgiveness of sins (Matthew 28:19-20, Acts 2:38).
3) Jesus is the head of the church, and we submit to him (Colossians 1:18).
4) We have leaders in the church and as they follow Christ, we submit to them (Hebrews 13:7, 17).

E. Lord of your dating life or marriage
1) How great Christian dating and marriage is! Both have a standard for purity.
2) Advice and help are needed to do it right and to keep it right.
3) Biblically you must marry only a Christian. Obviously you will marry someone you date; therefore, you date only Christians!
(Exception: An existing dating relationship—Handle with care and wisdom. Not a must to break up—a must to stop sin (if any) and a must to discipline it, and a must to make the decision that if the person is not really interested in becoming a Christian or is pulling the other person down spiritually, they will break it off immediately.)
4) 1 Corinthians 7:39: Disciples must marry in the Lord.
5) 2 Corinthians 6:14-18: There is no closer yoke than the marriage yoke.
6) Discuss any marriage issues such as changes, understanding roles, apologies, asking forgiveness, confessions, etc.

F. Lord of your job, profession or school
1) Ephesians 6:5-9: The slave/master is similar to the employer/employee or teacher/student relationship.
2) Work as if you are working for the Lord.
3) Excel without putting it in first priority.
4) Christians are to work and be responsible for their own needs. If a person does not have a job, it is his job to work eight hours a day to find one! (2 Thessalonians 3:10-13).

G. Lord of your relationships
1) Friends (1 Corinthians 15:33): Bad company corrupts good morals. And the opposite is also true, so your best friends should be those who are strong in following Jesus.
2) Family: Honor them but, at the same time, love them less than Jesus. You will always end up pleasing those you love the most! (Matthew 10:37).

H. Lord of your discipling
1) Discipling process is the forming of Jesus in you.
2) God disciples you (works in your life).
3) You must allow others to disciple you also; it's a privilege!
4) A discipling relationship is a great friendship with someone who is more like Jesus and

who can help, advise and instruct you in obeying God and becoming like Jesus.

5) Always use the Bible as the standard for right and wrong.
6) Discipling is God's idea. "Teach them to obey" (Matthew 28:20; Colossians 1:28-29; Proverbs 9:8; 11:14; 15:10; 15:12; 15:22; 20:18; 27:5-6; 27:17).
7) This relationship provides a way to obey all the "one another" Scriptures.

I. Lord in the midst of persecution
   1) 1 Peter 4:1-5: "They" are old friends and family and they think it strange to change your life for God. Your changed life may scare and convict the lives of others.
   2) 1 Peter 4:12-16
      a) People may use terms like "Bible banger," "Jesus freak," "cult" and "mind control."
      b) Persecution may come in the form of TV shows, newspaper articles, or exit counselors.
      c) Anything with commitment and religion is suspect these days. The core issue is having Jesus as Lord and obeying what God demands.
   3) You will be persecuted, but no one knows to what degree. You must be willing to die for Jesus. If you are willing to die, a little newspaper article with misinformation or twisted information will not stop you from following him!
   4) Persecution does not always mean a group is right with God, but where there is never persecution; it is a sure sign that something is wrong.
   5) Jesus was persecuted. His worst enemies were his fellow Jews.
   6) First-century Christians were persecuted. Why should it be any different now?

J. Lord of our talents and gifts
   1) Use your gifts to serve and help others, not just to advance your career or your self.
   2) Find out how you can use your talents to serve the kingdom and your local congregation.

K. Lord of our money
   1) 1 Timothy 6:9-10, 17-19
   2) You must be willing to no longer waste your money on sinful pursuits.
   3) It is a privilege to use it for good, for God's work!
   4) 2 Corinthians 9:7-8: Be ready to participate in the weekly contribution for the work of the church. 10% is a good place to start. (The Jews were commanded to give 10% of

everything; furthermore they had additional offerings throughout the year. How much more should disciples give!)

5) Never give out of compulsion. Plan it, decide it and then do it.
6) Give because of gratefulness for your salvation. You can never out give God! (Malachi 3:10).

3. Conclusion
   A. Jesus is to be Lord of all (Luke 9:24; Luke 14:33).
   B. Live your life asking, "What would Jesus do?" (Philippians 2:9-11).
   C. John 10:10b: Having Jesus as your Lord means having a deep, fulfilled and satisfying life now and eternal life later. Jesus never said it was the easiest life, but it is the best life!
   D. Are you ready to make Jesus the Lord of your entire life?
   E. Be urgent!

NOTES:

Counting the Cost

Introduction

A. This study is to help a person determine if he or she is ready to follow Jesus.

B. Nothing new should come up during this study. Everything should already have been discussed. The purpose of this time is to make sure that nothing has been missed and that the person is really ready to make Jesus his Lord and be baptized into Christ. (This general format should also be used for counting the cost with someone placing membership into the congregation.)

C. This should be done with an experienced spiritual leader.

1. Why do you want to become a Christian? Answer should include his love for God and gratitude for Jesus' death.

2. A. Please explain to me how to become a Christian.
   B. Please explain who is and who is not a Christian.

3. Are you ready to aggressively develop your personal relationship with God through daily Bible study and daily prayer?

4. Do you understand that there is only one church? Explain this to me.
   A. If you move, will you only move where there are disciples?
   B. Talk over any problem visa situations

5. A. Do you realize the commitment in our congregation?
   B. Are you committed to being there at the specific times when the body gathers? (i.e. devotionals, fellowship time, seminars, etc.)

6. Are you ready to repent of all of your sin? What will be the most challenging ones? Get specific.

7. Are you willing to make Jesus and his church first over friends and family?
   A. Are you ready for possible persecution/hardships/rejection?
   B. Are you ready to actively love your friends and family more than ever before?

8. Are you willing to excel in work/school without making it your first priority? Do you have any work conflicts with church right now? What is your solution?

9. Are you ready to put your love life (marriage or dating) into God's guiding hands?
   A. What specific changes are you making?
   B. What will your specific challenges be?

10. Are you ready, willing and happy to contribute toward the work and needs of the church?
    A. We recommend starting at 10%, but it is between you and God.
    B. Is your contribution sacrificial?
    C. Your giving demonstrates your faith.

11. Do you understand your new purpose in life when you become a Christian?
    A. You will be working to get people to the services.
    B. Will you set aside time for studying with non-Christians?
    C. Are you ready to begin (or continue) sharing with your friends and family?

12. Are you ready to have the mind-set of a disciple?
    A. Once a disciple, always a disciple. It is a lifetime commitment.
    B. Are you ready to be a learner your whole life?
    C. Are you ready to receive help from your new discipleship or one-another partner?
    D. Are you willing to be supportive and submissive to church leadership? (Ultimately, the Bible is the final authority.)

13. What will be your greatest cost/change/ challenge in becoming a Christian?

14. Are you ready and willing to make Jesus your Lord? Do you have a go-anywhere, do-anything, give-up-anything attitude?

15. Do you realize that from one perspective there is *really no cost?*
    A. The grace of God saves your completely.
    B. Grace saves you, not your works (i.e. you are saved for good works, not by good works).
    C. Do you understand that you work out of your love and appreciation for God and Jesus and all they have done for you?

Conclusion

A. At the end, discuss any concerns that have come up.
B. Have him think through any concerns you or he have via a walk, a prayer, etc.
C. Ask him when he would like to be baptized into Christ. Be urgent!

NOTES:

Deep Convictions

A thirteen-week study guide especially designed for the new disciple who seeks to build a powerful life in Jesus Christ and for the older disciple seeking to revitalize his walk with God.

Edited by
Tom Jones

Contents

Introduction

Most likely, this study guide is being given to you on the day of your baptism into Christ. If so, this day is, without question, the most important day in your life. This is the day for which you were born! The decision you have made to die with Christ in your baptism, accept his grace and put on his new life will affect every area of your life. As God's Word says in Colossians 3:3: "you died, and your life is now hidden with Christ in God."

The study you are about to begin is designed to help you develop deep convictions from God's Word each day for the next 13 weeks. It can also be used by those who have been disciples for a while to find "renewed life" through a return to the basics. As you begin this study to learn God's word, you need to understand how important this is for you. If you build a strong foundation now, it will serve you well for years to come.

Knowing the Scriptures is vital. They equip you for every good work (2 Timothy 3:1-7). Jesus was deeply committed to the Scriptures, using them powerfully in crucial moments in the spiritual battle. (Matthew 4:1-11 and Luke 4:1-13. With his example, Jesus shows us that we too need to love the Scriptures and use them daily. Jesus said, "Man does not live on bread alone, but on every word that comes from the mouth of God" (Matthew 4:4). Make up your mind that you will not let anything get in the way of your daily study of God's word. Your life depends on it.

For The Greatest Growth

1. *Buy a notebook and keep the notes that you will make as you go through this material.* Writing down your answers and thoughts will be very helpful to you. The better you learn these things now, the more effective you will be in sharing what you know with others.

2. *Have a regular time and place to do your study.* Pick both so that you will be as free as possible from interruptions and distractions. For those with normal schedules, early morning times are usually the very best.

3. *Read and underline, mark or somehow identify every scriptural reference in your study.* This will help you in remembering where passages are located and will give you one more way of being effective as Jesus' disciple.

4. *Have a great relationship with a more mature Christian who can check your progress as you move through the study.* Take advantage of all the help you can get. Be eager to receive instruction and correction. The crucial issues you will study out will serve you powerfully the rest of your life. You want to give this your very best.

5. *As you work on each lesson, write the current date in the space provided.* This will help you keep track of the consistency of your own pattern of study.

6. *Keep these notes and review these convictions.* Your own notes can become a valuable resource when you need encouragement in these areas and when you are sharing with others.

May God bless you with great times in his Word and may those times always draw you personally closer to him, enabling you to bring others to Christ.

Week One
MISSION

Therefore go and make disciples of all nations...

MATTHEW 28:19

You have just made the greatest decision a person can ever make. In your very first week as a disciple, you will study how God plans to use you to bring others to the new life you have found in Jesus Christ. The other studies that will follow will help prepare you for this mission, but it is good right at the beginning to understand what your exciting and fulfilling purpose is as a disciple of Jesus.

Day 1—Crucial Last Words

1. If you have not read the introduction of the previous page, please do so before you begin.

2. Before you actually begin this plan for Bible study, please take a few minutes to write in your notebook what your baptism into Jesus Christ meant to you. Why did you do it? What has changed because of your decision? Keep this statement in a safe place and refer to it often. Even as the years pass it will serve as a powerful reminder to you of the significance of your decision and of what you want to share with others.

3. The last words a person speaks usually tell us a lot about the major things on that person's heart. Turn to Matthew 28:18-20 and read again the final commission of Jesus Christ before he left this world.

4. What does it mean that Jesus has all authority over you? How do you feel about that? Where is he telling you that he wants you to "go?" What does he want you to do with the life he has given you? Who in your life heard Jesus say "go" and went to you? How do you feel about them because of it?

5. Jesus is sending you into your world to bring others to him. Write down the names of some of the people in your world right now that you want to be "going" to with his good news. Pray every day this week for them to be open to the gospel.

Day 2—Talking Babies

1. Begin by reading 1 Peter 2:2-3. Who are some of the people receiving this letter? In what way are you a "newborn baby?"

2. Now read 3:13-17 (especially looking at vv. 15 and 16). Does it seem that Peter thought the newborn babies should wait a while before sharing their faith? As a "newborn" what do you have to share with others?

3. Write down what you think is involved in each of these statements and why each is so important in making disciples.

a) "In your hearts acknowledge Christ as the Holy Lord."
b) "Always be prepared to give an answer."
c) "With gentleness and respect."
d) "Keeping a clear conscience."

4. Decide which friends on your prayer list that you will talk to about God and when you will do it. Pray for them specifically.

Day 3—The Committed

1. Begin today by reading the following passages from the Book of Acts:
   a) Acts 4:16-20
   b) Acts 5:40-42
   c) Acts 8:1-4

2. Write down what you see in these early Christians that impresses and convicts you.

3. Why do you suppose they were so committed to sharing the gospel with other people?

4. Opposition will always come to those who work to make disciples. You see it here in Acts. Read also Jesus' warnings in Matthew 10:21-25. Why would you expect negative reactions from some people as you share the message of Jesus? How will you respond?

5. Write down at least three different places where you will go today, and then pray about taking God's message into those places.

Day 4—Sharing Your Life

1. Read 1 Thessalonians 2:7-9 as Paul talks about the relationship he had with some that he had led to Christ.

2. What do we need to learn from Paul's example about how to reach out to other people?

3. What would be involved in "sharing not only the gospel with someone, but our lives as well?"

4. Someone once said :"People don't care how much you know, until they know how much you care." How can you show some of the non-Christians around you that you really care for them?

5. Read Matthew 25:31-36. How are other Christians around you seeking to fulfill this passage in their lives? Who can you talk with this week about this passage and how to live it out in your life?

6. Decide which friend you most want to reach out to and ask another disciple to help you develop a plan.

Day 5—The Love of Christ Compels

1. Read 2 Corinthians 5:11-21.

2. Write down at least five things this passage teaches about evangelism (sharing your faith).

3. Go back to 2 Corinthians 4:7-12. What do we need to learn from Paul's experiences in sharing the Word with people?

4. Read 2 Corinthians 4:1 and commit it to memory.

5. Why could there be no greater purpose in life than bringing others to Christ?

6. What great feelings do you have when you share your faith? What does it do for your convictions?

Day 6—Pray, then Proclaim

1. Begin today by reading Colossians 4:2-6.

2. List all the things you find here in regard to sharing your faith with someone.

3. What do you think Paul meant by "making the most of every opportunity?"

4. List some opportunities you could have used recently if you had been more alert and ready to speak.

5. Have you heard the term "lifestyle evangelism"? It refers to the fact that we should not reserve one night of the week for evangelism or even two or three, but that we should be living lives that are always evangelistic. What are some things that we need to be saying to ourselves at the beginning of every day in order to live an *evangelistic lifestyle?*

6. How will your lifestyle be evangelistic *today*?

Day 7—We Plant; God Makes It Grow

1. Read carefully Jesus' words in Mark 4:26-29.

2. Now turn and read Paul's words in 1 Corinthians 3:5-9.

3. What is our role in making disciples?

4. What is God's role?

5. Why can we never be prideful about the fact that we have been used to lead someone else to Christ?

6. If God is really the one who brings change to people's hearts and lives, why would he want us to share in the work?

7. Look back over the people and opportunities you have written about this week. Pray about these and commit yourself to be used for the rest of your life to bring other people to Jesus Christ. If reaching out is a big difficulty for you, admit that to someone and let them help you to overcome it. But believe that it can happen in your life! Look forward to being used in a great way.

8. Decide who you will reach out to next week and how.

Week Two
AUTHORITY

All scripture is God-breathed...
2 TIMOTHY 3:16

In your second week you will be studying passages that show the importance of living by God's word and no other authority. This is a deep conviction that you need to have in your heart and one that you need to pass on to others.

Day 8—The Final Authority

1. As you begin to live your life for God it is important that you begin studying God's word with the right type of respect and eagerness. Turn and read 2 Timothy 2:15. How can you be obedient to this scripture?

2. Read again Matthew 28:18. Write down what the authority of Christ now means in your life.

3. Turn to John 12:47-50. What happens to the one who does not accept the words of Jesus? What does God want for us? How do we find that?

4. It is important to remember that God's word is our authority. His word is our standard for living. It doesn't matter what people have taught you before or what "you" think; but rather, what is final is what God says. Write down a specific example of how this needs to work in your life.

5. Look back at the names of those you want to share with whom you wrote down last week. What have you shared with them? Are you praying for them daily?

Day 9—Ungodly Religion

1. Begin today by reading 2 Timothy 3:1-5.

2. What is the problem with the kind of religion or "ungodliness" described here?

3. Come down to 2 Timothy 4:1-4 and read another description of powerless religion.

4. Why would people ever substitute men's teachings for God's teaching on a given subject? How do you think this tendency might creep into your life?

5. Why would carefully following God's message lead to powerful religion as opposed to powerless religion?

Day 10—Skill Needed

1. Begin your study today by reading 2 Timothy 2:15. Take a few minutes and memorize this.

2. What do you believe God is communicating to you here?

3. Write a brief explanation of each of these statements:

   a) To handle God's word correctly we must have great respect for it.
   b) To handle God's word correctly we must spend time studying it.
   c) To handle God's word correctly we must share it with a godly attitude. (See 2 Timothy 2:24-26.) List both godly and ungodly ways in which we can share our faith.

4. In some translations this passage speaks of "rightly dividing the word of truth." This was once interpreted to mean we need to know the difference between the Old Testament Scriptures and the New Testament Scriptures. The verse certainly refers to more than this, but no one can handle the Word correctly without understanding the difference. What is the difference in the Old Testament and the New Testament? (Have a mature Christian check your answer.)

Day 11—Sound Doctrine

1. Read Romans 1:16-17. Before you start today's study, ask yourself: "Is anything hindering me from sharing the Word of God with my friends?" If there is something, then it needs to be put to death. Remember that it is God's word that has the power to save. Turn to 1 Corinthians 2:1-5 for reinforcement.

2. Turn to 1 Timothy 4:16 and write down what two things are necessary to save yourself and your hearers.

3. There is no power in the things we tell people if we are not living the life we proclaim. Let God's word *convict* people and let your life *convince* them that his Word is truth.

4. Read Titus 2:1. What is sound doctrine and how might you learn it? What is the attitude of so many "religious" people toward sound doctrine? Why is it important to learn exactly what God has commanded?

5. Read Titus 1:9. What will we be able to do by holding to sound doctrine?

6. Turn to 1 Timothy 6:3-5 and write down what this verse means to you. What is the connection between false teaching and a bad heart or a bad attitude? Why is keeping a pure heart so important in understanding God's word?

Day 12—The Powerful Word

1. Read 2 Timothy 3:16-17 and Hebrews 4:12-13. Make a list of all the things that God's word can do for you.

2. Not only is it important to know what God's word is, but it is equally important to do what it says. Turn to James 1:22-25.

3. What happens to the man who does what he has learned? God cannot use us if we do not do what he tells us.

4. The person who doesn't put God's word into practice will forget what he or she looks like. Write down some things that you know are right and that you intend to put into practice today.

5. Turn in the Old Testament to Ezekiel 33:30-33. You will not be able to understand the true meaning of God's word until you do what it says.

Day 13—"Seems Right" or "Is Right?"

1. Very often in the practice of religion people make a decision to do something because what they "think" seems more right to them than what God's word actually says. What warning do you hear for your life in Proverbs 14:12?

2. For an excellent example of this problem, turn to and read 1 Samuel 15:1-23.

3. Why were Saul's actions judged to be wrong? What was his justification for what he had done? Why was God not "won over" by his argument?

4. Write down some examples of how Saul's problem might be found in someone's life today.

5. In view of Saul's problem, what attitude do you want to have toward God's word?

Day 14—Building on a Rock

1. You have now been a Christian for two weeks. Write down some things you have learned and are wanting to do your third week as a Christian. Share these things with a brother or sister and let them help you and encourage you.

2. Turn to Matthew 7:21-27. Read this passage several times and write down what it means to you. Who are the people who will be turned away?

3. Now turn to Luke 6:46-49. What does Luke say about the one who builds his house on the rock?

4. The right attitude toward God's word is a crucial foundation for future growth. Read and memorize Psalm 1:1-3. It is so important to stay planted by the stream. Carry this Psalm in your heart, meditate on it often, respond to its challenge, and you will grow!

Week Three
GRACE

For it is by grace you have been saved.

EPHESIANS 2:8

"Amazing Grace" is not just a great song. It is one of the great themes of the Bible. We are saved by God's amazing grace. We are useful to God because of his amazing grace. We are to receive his grace with thanksgiving and with eagerness to let it change our lives.

Day 15—Lavished on Us

1. The grace of God makes our salvation possible. The grace of God also makes our growth and development possible. His grace is the source of everything that is good in us. Turn and read Ephesians 1:1-10. Mark each reference to the word "grace."

2. Grace is "giving to someone who deserves *nothing* as though he or she deserves *everything*," and that's what happens to us in Jesus Christ. We deserve *nothing,* but in him we are given *everything*. In spite of our sin, we are treated as if we were like Christ himself. This means we are judged not on the basis of our performance, but on the basis of grace. Incredible!

3. The NIV translation in 1:8 speaks of the grace God has lavished on us. What does the word "lavished" mean to you? What picture does that give you of God? How does this differ from some views of God that you may be familiar with?

4. What is Paul's response, described in 1:3, to such incredible grace? How should your understanding of God's grace change your attitude and outlook on life?

5. Spend some time just trying to comprehend how blessed you are to have been taught about the grace of God. Give praise to God with all your heart.

Day 16—Standing in Grace

1. Turn to Romans 5:1-11. Why is it so amazing that God has shown his grace to us?

2. In view of the teaching of this passage, why is it so foolish for us to ever be proud, arrogant or boastful in any situation or relationship?

3. In v. 2 he says it is in "this grace in which we now stand." Grace is a state in which you now stand and in which you will continue to stand as you continue in your faith. How does it give you security to know that you are standing (living) in a state of grace?

4. Suppose you fail in some way tomorrow and feel defeated. What difference will it make that in Christ you "stand in grace?"

Day 17—United with Christ

1. Read Acts 2:36-38 and then Romans 5:20-6:7.

2. Does baptism look like something that merits you salvation or is it the way God tells us to say "yes" to his grace, which we could never merit?

3. Write down what Romans 6 is saying happened to you in your baptism by the grace of God.

4. How does what happened (what God did) need to affect your attitude toward sin?

5. What is wrong with saying "let's continue in sin so grace can abound?"

Day 18 —Saved for Good Works

1. Read Ephesians 2:1-10.

2. Write a short explanation of each verse in this text.

3. Look carefully at v. 10. What is the whole purpose of grace? If a person does little or nothing as a disciple because "I am saved by grace anyway," what is he missing?

4. What good works do you see that God's grace has equipped you to do? What specifically are you wanting to do *today* out of appreciation for being saved?

5. If God has treated you with grace, how are you going to treat other people who sin and make mistakes? Read Ephesians 4:32.

Day 19—Grace that Teaches

1. Read Titus 2:11-14.

2. This passage could be translated "the grace of God gives us an education." What is the whole purpose of God giving us his grace?

3. List some things that the grace of God educates you to do.

4. Why must a "yes" to God's grace be followed by a "no" to worldly passions and ungodliness?

5. Is there anything still in your life that God's grace is teaching you to say "no" to?

6. Using your answer in question 5, now write out the following: "God's grace is sufficient to enable me to say "no" to...

Day 20—When We Sin

1. By today you have probably realized that you are not doing all for Jesus Christ that you determined to do almost three weeks ago. You want to love him with all your heart, soul, mind and strength. But you have failed in some specific areas. What you will study today will be very important in dealing with this for the rest of your life.

2. Turn to 1 John 1:5-10. Read it carefully.

3. Think of the difference in light and darkness. Think of the difference between a bright open room with lots of windows and a totally dark basement area. In one, things are out in the open. You can see them as they really are. In the other, things are hidden and covered by the darkness. With this in mind, what does John mean when he calls us to "walk in the light?" Do you see how this fits with v. 9 and the call to confess our sins?

4. We all—from the oldest to the youngest in Christ—sin. If we claim that we don't, we lie (v. 10). How, then, are we to handle all of this? Do we cover and hide our sins? Or do we bring them out into the open through confession?

5. Write down the two results of walking in the light as described in v. 7. Why is this passage comforting? What does it teach you about relationships in Christ?

6. Remember this: Satan's only ground is darkness. When we confess our sins and bring them out into the light, we take away from him his only base of operation, and we enjoy the power of God's grace and the blood of Christ continually cleanses us from all sin.

7. Have you been open about your sins? Has God forgiven you?

Day 21—Not Without Effect

1. Read 1 Corinthians 15:9-11.

2. In what sense can you say something similar to what Paul says in v. 9?

3. What do you think he means when he says "and his grace to me was not without effect?"

4. How can you respond so that God's grace will not be without effect?

5. Why do you think Paul adds that last comment in v. 10, "Yet not I. but the grace of God that was with me?"

6. End this week of study with time to thank God and praise him for his marvelous grace. Look at your lostness without him and his great mercy that you in no way deserved. Make sure there is no self-righteousness or arrogance in your heart but that you truly believe "by the grace of God I am what I am." Remember and write down where you were headed and what would have happened if you had not become a disciple. Share this with someone you want to be saved. Be a grateful Christian.

Week Four
DYING TO SELF

But if it dies, it bears much fruit...
JOHN 12:24 (RSV)

This week you will be studying passages in the Scriptures that show so clearly what the real problem in life is. The problem is the "old self" that lives for itself. Jesus Christ calls for the old self to be crucified, and he promises to raise up a new and very different "self." It is in dying that we find life.

Day 22—The Power of Dying

1. Turn to Luke 9:18-26. Read this passage through at least twice, underlining or making notes on what you believe are the key words and phrases. Write an explanation for verses 23, 24 and 25.

2. Now turn to Luke 18:28-30 and look at the promise that is given to those who accept discipleship. How do you expect this to work out in your life?

3. These two passages will become very important as you share your life in Christ with others. Why is this true? Remember where they are and think about how you should share them with someone else.

4. Be sure to spend time in serious prayer each day. Later in this study we will examine prayer, but don't wait until then to begin to develop a great prayer life. You are God's son or daughter and he wants you to talk with him.

Day 23—Co-Crucified with Christ

1. Begin today by reading Galatians 2:20. Take a few minutes to memorize this verse.

2. The word in Greek in this verse actually means "I have been co-crucified with Christ." How do we use the prefix "co?" What is a "co-leader" or "co-worker?" And so what is the message for Christians?

3. Among other things, the crucifixion of Jesus meant he voluntarily gave up his rights for the good of others. What "rights" do you think you might have a tendency to hold on to? How do you need to give them up for others?

4. The crucifixion of Jesus meant he put others' welfare above his comfort. How can you share in his crucifixion? What was the result of his crucifixion? What will be the result of yours?

5. Why is Matthew 7:12 a description of the "crucified life?" How are you making this part of your character?

Day 24—From Old to New

1. Turn again to Romans 6:1-4. Read and study this carefully. Each time you come to the word "we" or "us" substitute your own name. (For example, v. 2—"By no means. John died to sin; how can he live in it any longer?")

2. Write down some things about your old self that caused it to deserve death.

3. God has made you a "new self." How do you need to express your new self to others? How will they know you are *new*?

4. How do you specifically plan today to put v. 13 into practice?

5. Study Romans 6:15-23.

Day 25—Life in the Spirit

1. Before you start today's study, ask yourself a very important question: "Am I making every effort to be in close contact with other Christians?" This is crucial, and in Week Five the studies will all focus on the importance of relationships. Most of us have some tendency from time to time for various reasons to pull back from others. Spiritually, this can be fatal. Even when you don't "feel like it," stay in touch.

2. Turn to Romans 7:14-24 and read how powerless you are to live this new life without God's help. It is clear why we must "disown" the sinful nature. Especially note v. 24.

3. But now go on to Romans 8 where we see how we can do through Christ what is not possible alone. You were probably assured at your baptism into Christ that you would receive the Holy Spirit upon your obedience to the Gospel. Now study some of what that Spirit means in our lives. Read vv. 1- 17, making notes on the things that impress you the most. Remember to keep substituting your own name for pronouns.

Day 26—Taking Correction

1. As you have questions about things that you are studying or things that are happening to you, seek out some of your older brothers and sisters and let them help you. They have been through many things you will go through. Lean on their wisdom and understanding.

2. When we are children, we need to be taught things we don't know, and we need to be corrected when we are wrong. You are a baby in Jesus Christ. There is much you don't know and there are some areas where you need correction. That is true of every new Christian (and every older one!). *How you take correction is going to make all the difference in your growth in Christ.*

Turn to Proverbs 2:1-8. Next look at Proverbs 12:15. Go back to 10:17. What is the message? How does this relate to the idea that we have died to the old self?

3. Write down your own attitude toward being corrected. Distinguish between those things that are left over from your earthly nature and those things that Jesus Christ is putting in your heart. Read Proverbs 15:9-10 and 12:1.

4. Go to the New Testament now and read 2 Timothy 3:16-17 and answer this question: Why are other brothers or sisters to bring the word of God to you? What is going to be your attitude when they do?

Day 27—A New Attitude

1. Below are listed several verses. As you read them write down what you think the passage has to do with putting off the old self and putting on the new.
   a) Philippians 2:14-15
   b) Philippians 3:7-11
   c) Philippians 4:4
   d) Philippians 4:11-13

2. Write a response to the following statement: "In Jesus Christ we have all we need to maintain a great attitude." True or false? Why or why not?

3. What do these passages have to do with having a great attitude?
   a) John 16:33
   b) Romans 8:28
   c) James 1:2-4

4. What will be the effect on others when you allow God to give you a great attitude in all circumstances?

Day 28—Life from Death

1. Read John 12:20-26.

2. Notice in v. 23 that Jesus says the time has come for him to be "glorified." What do you think of when you hear that someone is about to receive "glory?"

3. In v. 24 Jesus most likely surprises his disciples. He indicates that the way he will find his glory is by becoming that seed that falls to the ground and dies. What does he say will be the impact of the seed that dies?

4. How do we know that this principle of being the seed that falls to the ground and dies applies to us who are disciples of Jesus? Particularly notice v. 26. Why is this an exciting principle?

5. In your life right now, who do you need to "die" for so they can become a disciple?

Week Five
FAMILY

Now you are the body of Christ, and each one of you is a part of it.
1 CORINTHIANS 12:27

This week you will study the importance of the church (the body of Christ, the family of God) and the relationships you will have in the church. This is what the kingdom of God is all about—relationships. To be righteous means to conduct your relationships (with God and with others) in the right way.

Day 29—Jesus' Church

1. Jesus Christ, who has all authority, taught us that the church is crucial in his plan. In Matthew 16:16-18, Jesus heard Peter confess him to be the Christ, the Son of God; and immediately Jesus said, "Upon this rock I will build my church, and the gates of Hades will *not prevail against it*." Jesus saw the church as the center of his plan. He wanted to build it and he intended to make it so strong that the forces of Satan could not stand against it. What Jesus counted as so important, we too must count as so important. What statements have you made or heard religious people make that discount (lessen) the importance of the church? What would Jesus say?

2. For a true picture of what the church should be striving to become every day, look at Acts 2:40-47. What impresses you the most?

3. What can you do today and the rest of this week to contribute to this kind of life among God's people (the church)?

Day 30—New Relationships

1. As you read each of the following passages, write down something the passage teaches that must be in our relationships in the Body of Christ.

   a) John 13:34-35
   b) Ephesians 5:1-2
   c) 1 Corinthians 13:1-3
   d) Colossians 3:14
   e) Galatians 5:6,13,14
   f) 1 Peter 4:8, 9

2. What does it mean to love another person?

3. What does 1 John 3:16 say it means to love another person? How does this apply to our relationships?

4. What is so good and so right about loving like this? What are the results?

5. Surprise someone today with a special act of love.

Day 31—Belonging

1. Paul describes the church as the "Body of Christ." Read Romans 12:1-8. How does giving yourself first to God need to lead to giving yourself to other people in the Body of Christ?

2. Notice particularly v. 5 which says, "each member belongs to all the others," or "we are all members of one another." How does this fit with or conflict with the often popular idea of individualism?

3. List three things that you already know you can do for other members of the Body of Christ. Share these with someone who is close to you and get his reaction.

4. List at least three things that you know you need from the Body of Christ in order to grow in Christ.

Day 32—Unity

1. Read Ephesians 4:1-5. Why does it seem to you that God is so very concerned about the Body of Christ having unity and peace?

2. Turn to Romans 14:13-15:3 and read how far we should go and how much we should bend to keep the Body of Christ together. Can you think of a practical application of this passage?

3. Is there anything in your life that is so important to you that you would not give it up even if it was keeping people from coming to Jesus Christ or growing in him? If there is, look back to v. 21 and get help in dealing with this area of your life. What most competes against Christ in your life and why?

Day 33—Purity

1. God is greatly concerned about the unity of the church. He is also greatly concerned about the purity of the Body of Christ. We are called to a holy life and a pure life, and sin in the Body that is being hidden or ignored will destroy the power of the church.

2. Read Ephesians 4:17-5:14. List those things which are described here as improper for God's holy people.

3. How would living as "children of light" be totally different from those things you have just listed? What is the basic difference?

4. You are a young Christian, but what should you do if you see brothers or sisters falling into sin? Read Galatians 6:1-2 and write out the principles you learned about who should help others with their sin and how it should be done.

Day 34—Encouragement

1. One of our greatest responsibilities is to *encourage* each other in the Body of Christ. Read an important statement about this in Hebrews 3:12-14.

2. According to this passage why is encouragement so needed? Judging from this passage, what kind of encouragement do you think would prove most helpful?

3. Look at Hebrews 10:24-25. What do we need to do to make our meeting times even more encouraging? Why is it discouraging for someone to miss meetings without communicating why they are not there or without getting advice?

4. Write down the names of three people you want to encourage and how you plan to do this.

5. Explain why different people are encouraged by different means.

Day 35—Conflict Resolution

1. The Body of Christ will not be a "perfect place" immune from relationship problems. Why will problems even arise in relationships that are in the church?

2. Read two important passages that tell us how to resolve problems that arise in the church.

a) Matthew 5:23-24 (Remember Jesus is teaching Jews here who still went to the temple to offer sacrifices; but what is the principle for us?)

b) Matthew 18:15-20

1) How is this different from the way people often handle a problem of sin? Why will step one work most of the time?

2) Why is step two sometimes going to be needed?

3) Why would the church have to sever fellowship with the person who will not repent and confess his or her sin?

3. Determine early in your Christian life that you will not complain or grumble behind someone's back. Determine that you will go to them and seek to resolve the problem with God's help.

4. You have been a Christian more than a month now. How would you evaluate the way you have handled your relationships in the Body?

5. Read 2 Corinthians 1:12. What are you appreciating about relationships that are based on God's grace and not worldly wisdom?

6. Ask someone close to you for some feedback on the conduct of your relationships so far.

7. Praise God for relationships based on Jesus and the grace of God.

Week Six
HEART

This week all of the studies will have to do with keeping our hearts pure before God and before one another. Probably you have already heard much about the importance of a great heart, but this study will help you see how to have such a heart and what the result of such a heart will be.

> *Above all, guard your heart,*
> *for it is the well spring of life.*
> PROVERBS 4:23

Day 36—God Looks at the Heart

1. Read Proverbs 4:23. How would you define the "heart" that the writer is describing? And what would it mean to "guard your heart? "Read Jeremiah 17:9-10. Why did God say this about our hearts?

2. Look at 1 Samuel 16:1-7. Particularly notice v. 7. In terms of religion, how might our "outward appearance" be different from what is really going on in the "heart?" But what is it that God is concerned about?

3. Have you been tempted so far in your new life to put on the outward appearance without having the heart? If so, how?

4. Read Psalm 139. Especially notice David's prayer for a pure heart in vv. 23-24 and then spend some special time praying about your own heart.

Day 37—Heart Change

1. All the great men and women in the Scriptures had to deal with their hearts, but no one shares his heart with us and his struggle for purity of heart more than David.

Psalm 32 and Psalm 51 were written by David and will be important in this week's study. Read them both carefully at this time. Make notes on those verses that seem most significant.

2. From these Psalms we can learn valuable lessons about how to come to purity of heart and how to keep the heart pure.

a) We must be willing to face our sin honestly and admit to ourselves what it is (51:3).
b) We must be broken over that sin (take seriously its effects) (51:17).
c) We must be willing to confess that sin (32:3-5).
d) We must be willing to accept forgiveness, once broken (32:11, 51:12-16).

3. Why can no one have and keep a pure heart without dealing with sin in a biblical way?

Day 38—Knowing Your Sin

1. Briefly review yesterday's study. Reread Psalm 32 and Psalm 51.

2. David struggled before he faced his sin. When are times you really don't want to face your sin? How do you usually avoid that confrontation?

3. What did David mean when he said God's hand was heavy upon him? What do you do when you feel the hand of conviction on you?

4. David said, "I know my transgressions." Are there any things in your life that you need to face honestly and say "I know that is my sin?" What will be the good of such honesty?

Day 39—Confession

1. Today's study is a continuation of the previous days. Without re-reading them, can you give a brief summary of the two Psalms (32 and 51) you have been considering?

2. When David saw sin in his life, he was broken and contrite over that sin. What does that mean?

3. David confessed his sin. Why is confession "good for the soul?" Why does it bring healing?

4. Who did David confess to? (If you said "God," think again. He wrote this Psalm of confession to be read and heard by all Israel.)

5. What did you learn earlier about confession from 1 John 1:9? Memorize this verse.

6. Look at James 5-16. You will be tempted to not let this be happening in your life, but you must remember how right it is. Also memorize this verse.

7. None of this is to write a rule that says "you must confess every sin to some other person." But isn't it clear God's people need to have a confessing attitude? Isn't it clear that hearts cannot be pure where there is hiddenness or deception?

8. What is your attitude toward confession? Do you see it as an opportunity or a burden?

Day 40—Good Fruits

1. The last several days you have studied ways to keep a pure heart. Now we want to turn specifically to the *results* or *fruits* of

pure heartedness. Again, let's consider what we learn from Psalms 32 and 51.

a) There is a great awareness of for giveness and salvation.
b) There is a thankful, rejoicing, sing ing spirit.
c) There is a great desire to share the joy of salvation and cleansing. Look back through these two Psalms and write down the verses that illustrate these points.

2. Which of these results do you see most clearly in your own life?

3. What's the problem when these fruits aren't seen?

4. Ask someone who is very close to you in the kingdom how they feel about your heart.

Day 41—Heart Maintenance

1. After doing the study on the heart this week, why would you say that our hearts *need continual maintenance*?

2. Look closely at 1 Timothy 1:5-7. What is implied in the phrase "wandered away from...a pure heart?"

3. Describe how this process of wandering away from purity of heart might happen in someone's life. Give some steps that might be involved.

4. What are three things you can regularly do to guard against this "wandering" in your own life?

Day 42—"Where is My Heart?"

1. Turn to Proverbs 4:23 and Jeremiah 17:9. Write out what these passages say and why you think they say it.

2. In your Christian life you will need to learn to diagnose different "heart" conditions. Study the following:

a) Hard heart—Proverbs 28:14
b) Unrepentant heart—Romans 2:5
c) Unbelieving heart—Hebrews 3:12

3. As you handle different situations in your life, learn to ask, "Where is my heart?" If you resist correction, ask "Where is my heart?" If you find yourself wanting to skip a meeting of the Body, ask "Where is my heart?" Why is it so dangerous to give in even a little to a bad heart?

4. Who is someone you know who strikes you as having a pure heart? What is it about them that you want to imitate?

5. What kind of heart did God promise to give us as we surrender our bad hearts? (See Ezekiel 11:17-19.)

6. What is the end result for the pure heart? See Matthew 5:8.

Week Seven
SUBMISSION

Submit to one another out of reverence for Christ.
EPHESIANS 5:21

This week you will study one of the keys to the Christian life. It is seldom understood and almost always rejected by those in the world, but it is something that you see perfectly in Jesus Christ, and it is something he wants to see consistently in us. It is the principle of submission.

Day 43 —Different Situations

1. On the first day of our study on this topic we want to look at the different places in Scripture where submission is called for. Look up the following scriptures and list those to whom we are to be submissive .

   a) James 4:7
   b) 1 Peter 2:13-18
   c) 1 Peter 3:1-5
   d) Ephesians 5:21
   e) Hebrews 13:17
   f) 1 Peter 5:5

2. Now, to the right of each of these categories that you have written down, write the name of someone to whom you should be in submission.

3. What are some of the major problems that you have with having a submissive attitude in these relationships?

4. Why does being submissive fit with what you know about the message of Jesus?

Day 44—A Matter of Attitude

1. As you study the biblical concept of submission, one of the most important things to learn is that God wants us to have a submissive *attitude*. He does not want us to submit with resentment, resignation, or bitterness. He does not want our submission to be legalistic. He wants it to come from the heart because of our trust in him, because of our confidence that he honors submission.

2. Submissiveness was an attitude found in Jesus. Read about it in Philippians 2:5-9. How do we see submissiveness in Jesus?

3. Again read about Jesus' submissive attitude in 1 Peter 2:13-21 (note particularly the first part of v. 13, the first part of v. 18, and v. 21).

4. Once we realize that Jesus Christ was the perfect model of submissiveness, we realize that submissiveness does not mean certain things. It does not mean: (a) lack of conviction, (b) silence, (c) violating your conscience, (d) weakness, (e) inferiority.

Instead submissiveness, as we see it in Jesus, does mean: (a) surrender of self-interest, (b) yielding of personal rights in order to benefit others, and (c) trusting God.

Some people think to submit means to do nothing, but we see in Jesus' life that submission meant trusting God and that is *hardly* "nothing."

5. In view of what we see in Jesus, which Christians should be submissive?

6. Ultimately, to whom are we to be submissive? Read James 4:7-8.

Day 45—Key to Growth

1. One of the things that all Christians need to be concerned about is their own personal spiritual growth. Why is submission such an important attitude to have in order for growth to take place? What will happen to the person who is unsubmissive?

2. Read Luke 2:51-52. Then go to Hebrews 5:7-9. How did Jesus learn what he learned?

3. What are some things that you are sure that God wants you to be learning right now, and how will a submissive attitude toward others help you to learn these things?

4. Do you feel like you have a rebellious or unsubmissive attitude about anything in your life at the present time? The tenor of God's word would strongly encourage you to open all that up to someone so you can more quickly deal with it and put it behind you. A rebellious attitude will destroy spiritual growth.

Day 46—"For the Lord's Sake"

1. Read 1 Peter 2:13 and then comment on each of the following phrases in that verse:

a) "submit yourselves"
b) "for the Lord's sake'
c) "to every authority instituted among men"

2. Is the following statement true or false? "Whenever we don't have a submissive attitude it is not for the Lord's sake but for our sake." Explain your answer.

3. Think of some times in your life when you were not submissive. How was your unsubmissiveness "for your sake" and not "for the Lord's sake?"

4. A man claiming to be a Christian once made this statement: "I submit to Jesus Christ and I submit to God, but any submission to men is way down the list, and I mean way down on the list." What do you think of his attitude? How does it fit with Scripture?

Day 47—Relationship with Leaders

1. In the Body of Christ God has placed certain men over you. First there are *elders (overseers)* in the body (see Acts 20:17; 28-31; 1 Peter 5:1-4) and then there are others who are over you because of special responsibilities they may have been given in the fellowship. Look at what Hebrews 13:17 says about your responsibility to these Christians.

2. Do you know the names of the elders and other leaders in the congregation where you are? Have you reached out to them in any way since becoming a Christian? How could you show them that you have a submissive attitude toward their leadership and that you want to make their work a joy and not a burden?

3. Does this passage say we have to agree with everything a leader does before we can submit to him and obey him?

4. Make sure your relationships with all your leaders are good ones. If there is ever any anger or resentment or hurt in you toward any of them, don't put off sitting down with that leader and opening up your heart. What would happen in a congregation if this did not happen?

Day 48—When We Must Not Submit

1. We must recognize that there will be times when we cannot specifically submit to people because to do so would be to be unsubmissive to God. Therefore, there are times when a Christian cannot submit. Turn to Acts 4:18-20 and Acts 5:27-30. Why did the early Christians not submit to the government in this instance?

2. Before we refuse to be submissive in any situation there are three important questions we need to ask ourselves:

a) Do I really want to have a submissive attitude or am I looking for an excuse to be independent and re bellious?

b) Is this really a violation of God's will or a violation of my strongly held tastes and preferences?

c) Am I not wanting to submit because of the principle involved or some person involved? (We should never decide not to submit to some one just because we have a negative personal feeling toward them.)

3. How could you refuse to submit to some particular thing, but still maintain a submissive attitude toward the person? Example: A Christian wife is asked by her non-Christian husband to lie for him to a business partner. How can she refuse but still maintain a submissive attitude toward her husband?

Day 49—The Blessings of Submission

1. After studying submission now for six days you should have a better picture of what true submission means, but read Philippians 2:9-11 to see the results of submission.

2. How did God bless the submission of Jesus Christ?

3. What are some specific ways that Christians will be richly blessed throughout the development of a submissive heart and attitude?

Therefore I will give him a
portion among the great,
and he will divide the spoils with
the strong,
because he poured out his life
unto death,
and was numbered with the
transgressors.
For he bore the sin of many, and
made intercession for the
transgressors
(ISAIAH 53:12).

Week Eight
THE FIGHT

For our struggle is not against flesh and blood...

EPHESIANS 6:11

For the next week you will be studying about the spiritual battle you are engaged in and how to have victory over sin. Every person must fight the sinful desires that war against our souls (1 Peter 2:11). But God has given plans and power to ensure our victory.

Day 50—Treating Sin Seriously

1. Read the following passages looking for God's thinking about sin: Matthew 5:29-30 and 18:6-7. What would you say is the first step in the fight against sin?

2. What does God feel about religion where sin is not treated seriously? Read Jeremiah 6:13-15.

3. Turn to Psalm 36:1-2. What is the problem with the man being described here? What attitude does he really need to have toward his sin? Also read Psalm 66:18.

4. Why do you think it is unlikely that you will ever have much victory over a particular sin in your life until you hate that sin?

5. Write down some sins that you have struggles with, and then write down why those sins need to be despised and hated. Write down the effects they have on you, others and God's plans.

Day 51—The Power of Repentance

1. Read 2 Corinthians 7:8-12. Paul describes here what happens when people take their sin seriously and have godly sorrow that leads to repentance.

2. What would be the difference in godly and worldly sorrow? Why does godly sorrow have such power and bring such results?

3. Using the diagram below as a model, write down a sin that you struggle with and the ways godly sorrow will lead you to demonstrate the attitudes that Paul describes.

God's Steps To Freedom—How To Change

(2 Corinthians 7:10-11)

REPENTANCE STEPS	SPECIFIC SIN
Earnestness (Sincerity)	Fits of rage. Galatians 5:19-20 I really intend to change & overcome. No excuses.
Eagerness to Clear Yourself	I will tell my closest brothers and my family my sin and my decision.
Indignation (Towards your sin)	I don't like myself when I lose control. I hate my anger.
Alarm (Urgency)	I must stop now. I cannot let this get any further.
Longing (Desire to be right with God)	James 1. I want my relationship with God to be right
Concern (For those you have hurt)	My anger scares my wife and my children & my friends.
Readiness to see justice done	I will give up whatever I need to in order to permanently change.

4. Retain this diagram and use it to help you make changes as you see other sins that need to be dealt with.

Day 52—The Power of the Word

1. What role does the word of God play in our fight against sin? Read Psalm 119:9-11, Matthew 4:1-11, John 8:31-34.

2. What attitude must one have toward God's word in order to use it for victory over sin?

3. Look back at the sins you listed in #5 on Day 50 and write down passages of Scripture that can help guard you against those sins. If you can't find what you need, ask someone for help.

Day 53—The Power of Prayer

1. What role does prayer play in the fight against sin? Read Matthew 7:7-11, Ephesians 6:10-18 (esp. v. 18), Hebrews 4:14-16.

2. As you pray about sin you are wanting to defeat in your life, what thoughts do you need to have about God? See the above verses and Romans 8:31-32, 1 John 2:1-2 and 3:1-3.

3. What does Jesus' example teach us about the kinds of prayers we may have to pray to win victory in our lives? Mark 1:35 and Hebrews 5:7-10.

4. In what ways have you been praying about sin you want to overcome? Who have you asked to pray for you?

Day 54—The Power of Relationships

1. What role does the Bible teach that we are to play in helping each other to live righ-

teously and stay out of sin? Read Galatians 6:1-2, Colossians 1:28-29,4:12, Hebrews 3:12-13, James 5:16.

2. List at least three ways that you need your brothers or sisters to help you guard your heart and your life from sin.

3. What does it say about us if we don't want help in overcoming sin, but only want to work on it by ourselves?

4. If there is some struggle with sin that you have not shared with another disciple, make a decision to do that today.

Day 55—No Temptation Too Great

1. Read 1 Corinthians 10:13. List the three promises God gives to us about overcoming sin in our lives. Why should it be such an encouragement to us to know that whatever temptation we face, it is common to man? Is there any temptation in your life that you have been reluctant to share with another Christian because you were afraid no one would understand?

2. You can see from this passage that we are not alone in our battle against sin. If you really believe that God has victory over Satan, you must not doubt the assurance of your victory over sin with God's help.

3. Read James 4:7-10. How would you describe the attitude that we are called to have here? What are some ways that you can practically come near to God?

4. How can you practically resist the devil when you face the temptation to:
   a) deceive?
   b) lust?
   c) have resentment?
   d) selfishly indulge?
   e) not care?
   f) speak unwholesomely?

Day 56—Never Give Up

1. In the struggle against sin why do you think we might be tempted to give up?

2. Why is it worth it to never give up? Study Romans 6:15-16; 8:18; 1 Corinthians 15:56; Galatians 6:7-10; 2 Timothy 4:7-8.

3. Read James 1:12. What do you think it means to persevere under trial? How do you know if you have stood the test? Describe some area in which you need to practice perseverance. Why will this challenge require perseverance?

4. Write down why you will never give up the fight against sin no matter how challenging it might become.

5. What decisions did you make this week about dealing with sin?

Week Nine
PRAYER

The prayer of a righteous man is powerful and effective.

JAMES 5:16

Today you begin your ninth week as a Christian. No doubt, prayer has become something very important to you, as it should be. Yet, even in this greatest of privileges you may have experienced struggles. Prayer is not natural, but like so many other facets of being a disciple of Jesus, it has to be learned. This week you will concentrate on prayer.

Day 57—Approach with Confidence

1. Think of someone in your life whom you can go to with confidence in any type of situation. How does that make you feel?

2. Read Ephesians 3:10-12 and Hebrews 4:14-16. These passages both use the word "confidence" to describe how we approach God. What does this mean to you? Of what can we be confident?

3. Why, as disciples of Jesus, are we able to come to God with such confidence?

4. When would be the only time that we could not be confident in coming to God?

5. As you pray today, thank God for Jesus who has made it possible for us to come to God without fear.

Day 58—Jesus: Man of Prayer

1. No one will have a meaningful prayer life who does not appreciate the importance of prayer and perhaps nothing helps us see this importance more than the life of Jesus. Read Luke 5:15-16; 6:12-13; 9:18; 11:1; Mark 1:32-36; and Hebrews 5:7-10.

2. Because of these statements about Jesus, G.S. Thompson has written: "Prayer was the atmosphere in which he lived. It was the air he breathed." Robert Coleman, commenting on the same scriptures, has written: "Prayer was indeed the sweat and tears of His ministry. The battle of the cross was fought and won on His knees." The same author also wrote: "Jesus never got behind in His work because He never got behind in prayer."

3. Write down what the example of Jesus means to you in relationship to your prayer life.

Day 59—Surrender

1. There are certain things necessary for effective, joyful prayer. For the next several days, we want to concentrate on some of these.

2. As a disciple what should be your main objective as you pray? Read carefully Matthew 26:36-44 and 1 John 5:14-15.

3. What is wrong if an attitude of surrender to God is not at the heart of our prayers?

4. Why did Hebrews 5:7 say that Jesus was heard by God? How can you tell if your prayers are unsubmissive prayers?

5. What prayers of surrender do you need to pray today?

Day 60—Faith

1. Another key element in prayer is faith. Prayer alone without faith has no effect (read Hebrews 11:6).

2. Read Joshua 10:12-14. Faith carries our prayers to the ears of God. God listened to a man—Joshua—because he prayed believing, and the sun and moon stood still. Joshua asked for something that was impossible, yet he asked the God who makes "all things possible."

3. Read again Mark 11:22-24. What doubts have you had as you prayed? What situations seem impossible? Where do these doubts come from?

4. Read Luke 18:1-8 and Psalm 34:15. When is it important to remember these passages?

5. Read James 1:5-8. What does this say to you?

6. List three things you want to pray about *with faith.*

Day 61—"Teach Us to Pray"
The disciples asked Jesus to teach them to pray. For the next two days we want to concentrate on some practical guidelines for prayer.

1. Read Matthew 6:5-8 and Luke 5:15-16. What do these passages seem to be telling you about prayer?

2. As you look at your living situation, what arrangements must you make to have a time and place to be alone with God?

3. Read Psalm 55:17. David prayed regularly. Jesus often withdrew to pray. Why is it important for you to have a regular, set time to pray? Why is it worth the extra effort to work this out?

4. Read Ephesians 6:18 and 1 Thessalonians 5:17. Prayer is not limited to a set time and place, but should be spontaneous and continuous throughout the day. Why does God want us to *"pray continually?"* What does this mean to you? How might such a thing be done?

Day 62—Pray Like This
1. Read the prayer in Matthew 6:7-13.
2. List the several different elements that make up this prayer. Which of these do you focus on regularly? Which do you tend to neglect?

3. Many times our prayers are concentrated on asking for certain needs to be met. Jesus teaches us to first of all focus on God and give him the honor and praise he deserves.

4. Do you have difficulty praising God? If so, use the Book of Psalms to train you. Start out with Psalm 24. Read it aloud.

Day 63—The Joy of Prayer
1. If we are to pray powerfully we must not only see the importance of prayer and the need for surrender and faith in prayer, but we must appreciate the joy of prayer. Read Philippians 1:3-6; 4:47 and 1 Thessalonians 5:16-18.

2. Why should your prayer life bring you joy? Can it do this even in the midst of trials?

3. What are some possible things that are wrong if a Christian does not see prayer as a source of joy?

4. As you close this week of study on prayer, what patterns of prayer do you have in your life at this time? What changes do you want to make?

Week Ten
DISCIPLINE

Run in such a way as to get the prize.
1 CORINTHIANS 9:24

This week of your study will be devoted to the area of discipline. This is an important part of doing the will of God in the most effective way possible. Disciplined Christian living is...*bringing all the areas of our lives under the control of Jesus Christ so that* all we do *fits together and contributes to our one purpose: to bring glory to God.*

When you became a Christian it was a decision to be a disciple of Jesus Christ, to put yourself under his discipline.

Day 64—The Spirit of Self-Discipline

1. Read 2 Timothy 1:7. What kind of spirit has God given us? What kind of excuses do you sometimes give for being undisciplined? Are they valid?

2. With the promise of this kind of spirit you can believe that you can become a disciplined person no matter where you are right now. Decide that from this time forward whatever changes need to be made will be made.

3. Turn to 2 Timothy 3:16-17. What part do the Scriptures play in becoming disciplined?

4. How could a failure to be disciplined in your study of the Scriptures affect being under God's discipline or control in other areas?

5. What kind of disciplined study do you want to have after this thirteen-week study is over?

Day 65—Not "Running Aimlessly"

1. Read 1 Corinthians 9:24-26.

2. What are some characteristics of discipline?

3. What is the purpose of discipline?

4. What are some characteristics of being undisciplined?

5. What does it mean to "run aimlessly?"

6. Are there any ways right now that you may be "running aimlessly?"

Day 66—Guarding Against Excess

1. There are any number of things that are not wrong in and of themselves, but to do them in excess without God's control will have a negative effect on your life and outreach.

2. What example of this does Paul give in 1 Timothy 6:6-10?

3. In the past what have been some things you might have done in excess without proper control or discipline?

4. Are there some things in your life right now that are not wrong but which could be done excessively if you are not careful?

5. Meditate on what your life would look like with the different areas under control. Get the image fixed in your mind. Now pray for God to give you the power to make that

a reality. Make sure you really want it before you pray.

Day 67—Mastered by Nothing

1. Read 1 Corinthians 6:9-20. As you read keep in mind that "everything is permissible for me" and "food for the stomach and the stomach for food" were popular proverbs of the loose-living Corinthian culture that these Christians were living in.

2. What is Paul's response to each of the popular proverbs?

3. Why must disciples make the decision to "not be mastered by anything"? What will be the result if we do not?

4. What in your life right now is "mastering you" or threatens to "master you?"

5. Make a time to pray with someone about this, this week.

Day 68—Learning from the Soldier, Athlete & Farmer

1. Read 2 Timothy 2:1-7 and look for the three analogies Paul uses to characterize the Christian life.

2. What discipline is involved in being a soldier that we need in Christ?

3. What discipline is involved in being an athlete that we need in Christ?

4. What discipline is involved in being a successful farmer that we need in Christ?

5. As we seek to be disciplined like a soldier, an athlete or a farmer why do we need to keep an eye on v. 1 and remember the grace of God?

Day 69—Spoiling the Fruit

1. Read and study Galatians 5:22-23.

2. Consider how the last element mentioned (self-control) relates to the others.

a) Why will a lack of self-control (self-discipline) hinder your ability to *love?*

b) Why will a lack of self-control interfere with *peace?*

c) Why will a lack of self-control often frustrate your ability to be *kind, patient and gentle?*

3. Self-control is a part of the fruit of the Spirit, so that means we don't produce it on our own. What attitude must there be in our lives if God is to produce this in us?

Day 70—Discipline & Emotions

1. Self-discipline not only applies to how we use our time, money and possessions. It applies to how we handle our emotions.

2. List three emotions that need to be controlled and disciplined in your life. Find scriptures that relate to each one.

3. Turn to and read Hebrews 11:8. What emotions could have controlled Abraham in this instance? How does *faith* bring those emotions under control?

4. Consider these same questions as you read Hebrews 11:17-19.

5. Someone has said: "We lose control when we take control. In the same way, we gain control when we give it to God." How does this need apply to your life?

Week Eleven
MONEY AND MARRIAGE

Marriage should be honored by all.... Keep your lives free from the love of money...
HEBREWS 13:4-5

In one passage the writer of Hebrews gives instructions about two key subjects for disciples: money and marriage (Hebrews 13:4-5). He realized that these were two areas that must be brought under the Lordship of Jesus. This week we will focus on those two areas. Money concerns us all. God's plans for marriage need to be understood whether or not we are currently married.

Day 71—The Necessity of Work

1. Money is not an evil. It is a necessity and the Scriptures teach that it should be honestly earned. Read Ephesians 4:28, 2 Thessalonians 3:6-15 and 1Timothy 5:7-8.

2. What attitudes did you have toward money before becoming a Christian? What changes have you had to make?

3. What is the impact of the irresponsible person who does not do his or her best to provide for financial needs?

Day 72—The Love of Money

1. Read Hebrews 13:1-5. We all must deal with money, but what attitude must we be careful not to have? Why is the love of money at cross purposes with following Jesus?

2. Read 1 Timothy 6:17-19. We are "rich" when we have the ability to meet our basic needs and then have money left over that can either be used to give us luxuries or help others. Most of us are in this category. From v. 18 write down three or four things we should do with our "discretionary money."

3. If we are not disciplined in the way we handle money what will happen to our ability to share? Who will we not be able to share with?

4. Read Romans 13:8. Unmanageable and unresolved debt is a major problem for many people in our world. What is to be the disciple's attitude toward debt?

5. Write down at least three negative effects that will be present when we have a problem with debt.

6. What were your financial habits before becoming a Christian? What changes have you made? If your financial house is not in order, if debt is a major factor in your financial picture, do not wait any longer to get help. Tell one of your leaders you need to talk. God can help you to victory if you are humble and open.

Day 73—Righteous Use of Money

1. In this study we want to look at two places our money needs to go as disciples of Jesus. First read Luke 14:12-14 and Matthew 25:31-46. How important is it to God that we give to the poor? In what ways can you do this right now? If you just don't know where to begin, ask someone for advice. Find out what organized efforts there are in your congregation. But whatever you find, do it.

2. Read Philippians 4:14-16. Paul describes here the way the church in Philippi supported him as he spent his life spreading the gospel of Jesus. It is right for those who have received instruction in the Word to support those who bring the Word to them (Galatians 6:6). Without the generous giving of Christians we would not have seen the gospel taken around the world in recent years. Without continued generous giving, we will not see the mission completed.

3. How much of your income is being used to help the poor and to spread the gospel? God's Old Testament people under a far less glorious covenant were required to give 10% and beyond. What would faith lead you to do today under the covenant brought by Jesus?

Day 74—Generosity

1. Read 2 Corinthians 8:1-7. What would be necessary for someone in extreme poverty to "well up in rich generosity"? What steps would enable *you* to become more generous in your giving?

2. According to 2 Corinthians 9:6-11 what will be the joys of generosity?

3. How are you making your decisions about your giving? Do you see your giving as being generous? What sacrifices would you have to make to be more generous?

Day 75—Marriage in a New Light

1. For the rest of this week we will focus on marriage. Read Genesis 1:26-31 and 2:15-25.

2. Who is the designer of marriage? What did he plan for the marriage relationship?

3. What happens today when people forget that God is the originator of marriage? What problems does that lead to? What does it have to do with the divorce rate in most countries of the world?

4. If you are married, what do you have now that you are a Christian that you did not have before becoming one? How are you letting it change your outlook on your relationship?

Day 76—A Perfect Plan

1. Read Ephesians 5:21-33. What is *God's* plan for marriage?

2. Why is v. 21 such a crucial introduction to this section?

3. If the wife follows God's plan for her and the husband God's plan for him, write out what kind of interaction this will lead to.

4. True or false? A husband or wife is relieved of his or her responsibility here if the other person does not hold up their end of the bargain? Explain your answer.

Day 77—Honoring Marriage

1. Read 1 Peter 3:1-7. What would you say the basic message here is for the wives? For the husbands?

2. If you are married, how does this passage personally challenge you? Share that conviction with your spouse.

3. Read 1 Corinthians 7:1-6. The Christians in Corinth were thinking that they might have more "spiritual" marriages if they refrained from the sexual relationship. What was Paul's answer? What attitude is he saying each marriage partner should bring

to the sexual union? For more on the biblical view of sex in marriage read Song of Songs in the Old Testament.

4. Read Hebrews 13:4. In what way can you give honor to marriage if you are married? If you are not?

Week Twelve GROWTH AND DIRECTION

I press on toward the goal.
PHILIPPIANS 3:14

In this week you will be studying passages from God's word that will help you keep on growing as a disciple, help you learn to discern God's will and help you make spiritual plans that God can bless.

Day 78 —Keep on Growing

1. Many seem to believe that the normal thing is for a person to grow as a Christian to a certain point and then level off. Read the following passages and see what you think:
   a) Hebrews 5:11-14
   b) 2 Peter 1:5-8
   c) 1 Peter 2:1-2
   d) 2 Peter 3:17-18

2. Look at Ephesians 3:14-19. How much is there to know? Who has learned enough?

3. It has been said that as Christians we either grow or dry up. Do you think this is true and if so why?

Day 79—Going After It

Spiritual growth is something you must go after. The following are four keys to growth:

1. *Make a Decision To Grow.* Very seldom does any significant growth occur without this decision. Read Philippians 3:7-12. What is Paul's attitude toward growth? Notice especially vv. 10 and 12. How are you answering this question right now: "In my own life, what am I willing to give up in order to grow?"

2. *Concentrate On Specifics.* Change takes place not in the vague or general but in the specific. "I want to be like Jesus." Okay! But how?

3. *Push Yourself To Grow.* We need to be so willing to put ourselves in situations where we must grow and where we must depend on God for his help. Read 1 Timothy 4:7. Why is the word "train" an important word here? When an athlete trains what does he do? What are some ways you can be pushing yourself to grow right now? (Think about areas where growth does not at all come naturally for you.)

4. *Have A Vision For What You Can Become.* Read 2 Peter 1:3-11 and realize that you can become everything that Jesus would have you to become. What is the promise that we have in v. 3? End your time today by reading Philippians 1:6.

Day 80—Not Growing? Take Inventory

1. If we are not growing then what does that mean? Read each of the following passages and complete this statement for each:

If I am not growing then it may mean that ...

a) John 12:24
b) Ephesians 4:15
c) Philippians 3:12-14
d) Hebrews 12:1-2
e) 1 Corinthians 9:19-23

2. Which of these passages most describes something that is holding growth back from you? Share your conviction with someone today.

(Note: Look ahead to Day 85 in your study and make sure you can get one of the items mentioned in point No. 1 by the time you reach this point in your study.)

Day 81—Knowing God's Will

All of us make plans. Hopefully we have some dreams for our lives.... goals. How can we know whether or not we're doing God's will? How can we know that decisions we are making align with God's will? The next four studies will deal with this topic.

1. Read Romans 12:1-2. What does this passage teach about knowing God's will? The word here for transformed is the word "metamorphosis." The usage of this word implies a radical or drastic kind of change. What are some ways in which God has had to radically change you in order to make known his will to you?

2. Read 1 Thessalonians 5:16-17. Sometimes God's will is difficult to discover in our lives but always we know some right things to do. It is always right to be joyful, to pray continually and to give thanks. Think back over the last week. Are there some times when this was not your attitude? Why will this attitude help you see other aspects of God's will?

3. Read Ephesians 5:8-17. How does tolerating darkness in our lives keep us from knowing God's will? Why are we being foolish?

4. Read Philippians 1:9-11. If we want to discern what is *best* then we must be letting our love abound more and more. So often, when we are struggling, when we have doubts or questions, when we don't know what God is trying to say to us, the best thing we can do is look for a way to serve someone. In what ways can your love abound more and more?

Day 82—The Importance of Plans

1. Read Psalm 20:1-5. From v.4 we can draw two conclusions:

a) God wants his people to have plans.
b) When his people have godly plans, he wants to bless those plans.

2. Why do you think that many religious people have no real plans for their spiritual development, but at the same time have various plans for other aspects of their lives?

3. If we don't have plans, then obviously God cannot make those plans succeed. It is, of course, possible to over-plan or to plan so much you can't possibly get to it all. But we all need plans—plans that God can bless. Write down elements in your plan for future growth in God's Kingdom.

Day 83—The Desires of Your Heart

1. Psalm 37:1-11. Look especially at v. 4 and make a list of the desires of your heart that you know are God's desires as well.

2. Look at v. 5. Can you give some specific examples of how you need *"to commit your way to the Lord?"* What is the promise made to you in v. 6?

3. Look at v. 8. What kind of problems do you get into if you begin to "fret" over your plans?

4. Describe the difference you want your faith to make in your life—as you make decisions and go through trials.

Day 84—Your Heart at Peace

1. Read Philippians 4:4-7. What words do you read here that relate to your life?

2. What is Paul saying that we can do once we have committed our present and our future to God? What is he saying God will do for us once we have made that commitment?

3. As you seek to grow and please God with a lifetime of service, you will be challenged. There will be hardships. There will be pain. There will be trouble. But look at what Jesus said about this in John 16:33. Life is difficult. Right? But what else is true?

4. Read about the ultimate result of your growth as a Christian in Romans 5:1-5. In what way will our "hope" not disappoint us? Read 1 Peter 1:3-5.

Week Thirteen
HOW TO STUDY

A STUDY OF COLOSSIANS

Let the word of Christ dwell in you richly.

COLOSSIANS 3:16

As we come to the last week of this guided study, the Letter to the Colossians has been selected for in-depth study. The study you do this week will give you a vision for the kind of study you can regularly have taking other books from the Bible as the object of your study.

Day 85—Introduction & Background

1. From a study Bible, Bible dictionary, or commentary read about the background of Colossians. Understand what concerns motivated Paul to write this letter.

2. Read Colossians 1:1-8 underlining key phrases as you read.

3. a) What qualities did Paul see in the lives of these Christians that caused him to be so thankful for them?
   b) Where did he see these qualities coming from?
   c) How are you showing these qualities in your relationships with others?

4. Read 1:9-14, underlining key phrases as you read.

5. a) List the things Paul was praying would be found in the lives of these disciples.

b) What kind of life is pleasing to God in every way? Where is your heart in regard to these things?

6. What overall purpose do you think Paul had in writing what he did in the introduction to this letter (vv. 1-13)?

Day 86—The All-Sufficiency of Jesus

1. Read Colossians 1:15-18, underlining key phrases.

2. Knowing the Colossian Christians may be under the influence of those who have an inadequate view of Christ, what message is Paul wanting them to understand about Jesus Christ?

3. Given what Paul says here, what understandings of Jesus are totally inadequate?

4. What is the personal significance of v. 17 for your life? How do you share this with other people who know you?

5. Read 1:19-23, underlining key phrases.

6. a) God wants to "reconcile" all of us to himself (vv. 19 and 22). What does this mean God really wants from us?
   b) How does the price he was willing to pay for such reconciliation need to affect us?
   c) From v. 22, what impact does it have on you to know that you can stand before God through Christ *"without blemish and free from accusation"?*
   d) According to v. 23, what is the key to remaining in such a state?

7. Read 1:24-27 and continue in your readings to underline key phrases.

8. What impact does the idea of *"Christ in you"* have on your life?

Day 87—A Heart for Others

1. Read Colossians 1:28-2:15.

2. a) What passion did Paul have? For what goal was he giving all he had, as God blessed him?
   b) How does God want to use you in the same way?
   c) What will you do today to fulfill this passage in your life?
   d) How will you let others help you toward being "perfect in Christ?"

3. a) Paul talks in these verses about "struggling" for his brothers and sisters. What struggles will we have to willingly accept in order to help others get where they need to be?
   b) What is the secret to Paul's ability to keep up the struggle?

4. a) Read 2:6-15 and start taking care ful note of the false ideas of which Paul is warning the disciples to be aware.
   b) Someone is probably telling the Colossians that they need Christ *plus* philosophy for the full life. What is Paul's answer and warning?
   c) What such philosophies are trying to influence you?

5. From vv. 9-15, why would you say you do not need Christ *plus* anything else to find your life?

Day 88—Watch Out for False Teaching

1. Read Colossians 2:16-23, looking for other misleading teachings that the Colossians were being tempted to fall into. Look for at least three major false teachings.

2. What do vv. 16-17 say to the person today who thinks we should keep the Sabbath and observe Old Testament regulations?

3. What is the basic problem with the person described in v. 18?

4. Does the word "asceticism" have meaning to you? If it does not, look it up in a dictionary.

5. Apparently some were teaching that asceticism was the way to spirituality—denying our bodily needs and harshly treating the body (vv. 20-23). What does the Bible say?

6. Why do you think people are often vulnerable to exotic teachings about how to become spiritual? What do they fail to understand about Christ?

Day 89—Off with the Old, On with the New

1. Read Colossians 3:1-17.

2. What reason does Paul give in vv. 1-3 for living a new and different life?

3. What things that *"belong to your earthly nature"* still need to be "put to death?" What does that language communicate to you? Dare you be that radical?

4. Of the qualities listed with which to *"clothe yourselves,"* which one is most missing from your present character or lifestyle? Do you believe God can add it to your life? Do you want it? What do you plan to do? Why?

Day 90—Everyday Relationships

1. Read Colossians 3:18-4:2. Compare with Ephesians 5:21-6:9.

2. What do all these things talked about here have in common?

3. Why is it so important that these relationships we are in, usually on a daily basis, be conducted so differently?

4. How many of these are specifically addressed to you and how can you demonstrate the spirit that Paul describes in these relationships? (Realize the master/slave directives are parallel to employer/employee or teacher/student relationships.)

5. Why does God give us instructions like this? What will be the results of obedience?

Day 91—For the Rest of Your Life

1. Read Colossians 4.

2. Earlier you studied vv. 2-6. Go back to your notes on Day 6 and see what you wrote down. What do you think you have learned about this in the last 12 weeks?

3. Why is Epaphras a great example for us? What characterized his approach to prayer? Why is his approach to prayer often a necessary one? What are some issues in your life that require nothing less?

4. Write out v. 17 putting your name in where you see the name "Archippus." How would you respond to receiving such direction from an apostle. How does it make you feel?

5. This is the last day of your guided study. At this point you need to formulate plans for continuing your own personal Bible study. There are many ways for you to proceed. One suggestion is to pick a certain gospel, letter, etc., and work your way through it verse by verse. Use the type of study done in Colossians and study books like 1 John, 1 Peter or Phillipians in the same way. Perhaps you want to study a certain theme in the Bible like "trust" or do some character studies of men and women in the Bible.

6. Whatever you decide to do, have a specific plan. Beware of the "lucky dip" method that involves just letting the Bible fall open somewhere each day. That may be often used but it is unproductive. Write down what you plan to study next.

As you leave this study, you should not think that you are through looking at these ideas. You will need to come back to them again and again. Many have worked through this material after being Christians and then have done it again a year or two later, finding that after a time of growth the concepts get even richer.

May God bless you in your future study of his will for your life! Make being with God every day for the rest of your life a joyful habit that you would not think of living without!

As a deer pants for streams
of water,
so my soul pants for you, O God.
My soul thirsts for God, for the
living God.
When can I go and meet with
God?

PSALM 42:1-2

Prepared to Answer
Chapter Summaries

Prepared to Answer by Gordon Ferguson deals with the contrast between various popular doctrinal positions and the actual teachings of Scripture. At the end of each chapter he includes summaries of material covered. These summaries are reprinted here. For much more thorough discussions, readers should consult *Prepared to Answer* available from Discipleship Publications International.

CHAPTER ONE

The Falling Away Was Foretold by God

The Plan:

1. The unity of everyone who desires to follow Christ is the will of God (John 17:20-23).
2. The word of God must be the basis for this unity (Matthew 7:13-14, 21; John 8:31-32; 17:17).

The Warnings:

1. Jesus said that many would lose their love for him and for others within about 40 years from the time he spoke (Matthew 24:10-12).
2. From among the true church, false leaders would arise soon after Paul left Ephesus (Acts 20:29-30).
3. False leaders would reach the point where they would assume position and power reserved only for God himself (2 Thessalonians 2:1-8).
4. The Holy Spirit was quite clear about the impending apostasy, which would include teachings forbidding marriage and the eating of certain foods (1 Timothy 1-4).
5. The time would come when men would seek false teachers who would water down the truth, in order to make them comfortable in their sins (2 Timothy 4:1-4).
6. False teaching is often motivated by greed (2 Peter 2:1-3).
7. The Antichrists were already teaching false doctrines about the nature of Christ in the first century (1 John 2:18; 4:1).

The Hope:

1. The Word of God is the seed of his kingdom (Luke 8:11), and when we plant it in the hearts of people today, it will produce exactly the church that Jesus built.
2. Jesus is the head of his one body (Ephesians 1:22-23; 2:16; 4:4), and he promised to save all of those who are in that one body (Ephesians 5:23).
3. Paul expected Christians to be perfectly united in mind and thought (1 Corinthians 1:10-13). In the remainder of the chapter, Paul shows that this remarkable unity occurs when Christ and his wisdom become the most important thing in all of our hearts.

CHAPTER TWO

Authority in Religion: From God or from Men?

1. *Catholic Claim:* the Bible cannot be understood by the average person.
   Bible Truth: John 8:32; Acts 17:11; Ephesians 3:3-5; 5:17; 1 Timothy 2:4.
2. *Catholic Claim:* the Bible plus Traditions are needed to find salvation.
   Bible Truth: Matthew 15:7-9; John 16:13; 2 Timothy 3:16-17; 2 Peter 1:3; Jude 3.
3. The truths of the Bible were revealed by the Holy Spirit to inspired prophets (John 16:12-16; Ephesians 3:3-5; 2 Peter 1:21; 1 Corinthians 2:13).
4. The Bible is precise in its accuracy (John 10:35; Matthew 22:23-33; Galatians 3:16).
5. It must be followed very carefully (Matthew 7:13-14, 21; John 15:10; Galatians 1:6-8; 2 John 9).

6. If the Bible cannot be understood, then either God did not want us to understand (but 1 Timothy 2:4), or he was not powerful enough to make it understandable!
7. Without understanding and responding to the Bible's message, we cannot go to heaven (Luke 6:46; John 8:32; Hebrews 2:9 and 5:9; 1 Peter 1:22).

CHAPTER THREE
The Exaltation of Men

1. *Catholic Claim:* The Pope is the visible head of the Church.
   Bible Truth: Jesus is the only head of the Church, and all Christians are the members of his spiritual body (Ephesians 1:22-23; Colossians 1:18-24).
2. *Catholic Claim:* The Pope is for all intents and purposes to be worshipped by his subjects (bowing down, kissing ring, etc.).
   Bible Truth: Paul refused worship (Acts 14:11-15) as did even an angel (Revelation 22:8-9).
3. *Catholic Claim:* Peter was the Rock on which the church was built.
   Bible Truth: Jesus was the Rock (the *Petra*, not *Petros*)—1 Corinthians 3:11; 1 Peter 2:4-8.
4. *Catholic Claim:* Peter was the first Pope.
   Bible Truth: There is not the slightest evidence that Peter was viewed in this way in the first century. The concept of the Papacy did not develop for three hundred years. Peter had less influence over the whole church than Paul had, for Paul was the apostle to the Gentiles, which was the larger group (Galatians 2:7-9). Also, Peter wrote only two brief books of the NT, while Paul wrote at least 13, including the one to the Roman church.
5. *Catholic Claim:* The Priesthood is based on apostolic succession.
   Bible Truth: A succession of apostles is impossible because of the qualifications in Acts 1:21-22.
6. *Catholic Claim:* Only special clergymen are priests.
   Bible Truth: All Christians are priests (1 Peter 2:5,9).
7. *Catholic Claim:* Saints are highly unusual spiritual people, usually canonized after their death.
   Bible Truth: All Christians are saints (Romans 1:7; 15:25-26—note in v. 26 that all Christians in Jerusalem were not poor, but all were saints).
8. *Catholic Claim:* Mary was a perpetual virgin.
   Bible Claim: She had other children (Mark 3:32; 6:3).
9. *Catholic Claim:* She never committed any sins.
   Bible Claim: She was a normal sinner like all humans (Romans 3:23), and at least once, she was very weak in faith toward Jesus and his mission (Mark 3:20-21, 31-35).

CHAPTER FOUR
Spiritualism Versus Faith: Coming To Christ

1. *Catholic Claim:* Man can and must merit grace and work off sins.
   Bible Truth: We cannot merit grace, and if we try to serve God while relying on

performance, we rule out grace (Luke 17:10; Romans 4:1-8; Galatians 3:10; Ephesians 2:8-10).

2. *Catholic Claim:* Salvation is very insecure, and purgatory necessary to pay for all of your sins.
   Bible Truth: If we are in Christ, there is no condemnation (Romans 8:1), our sins are continually cleansed (1 John 1:7-9), and none of them is even placed on our record (Romans 4:8). Salvation is *complete* (Romans 7:25).
3. *Catholic Claim:* The sin of Adam is passed on to every person (called *original sin*).
   Bible Truth: We suffer the consequences of Adam's sin, physical death (Genesis 3:22-24; Romans 5:12; 1 Corinthians 15:21-22). We cannot inherit his guilt (Ezekiel 18:20) for our spirits come directly from God (Zechariah 12:2; Ecclesiastes 12:7; Hebrews 12:9).
4. *Catholic Claim:* Infants need to be baptized because they are guilty of Adam's sin.
   Bible Truth: Baptism is always a response of faith and accompanied by repentance (Acts 2:38; Colossians 2:12). Babies do not need to be baptized to be saved, because they are already safe (Matthew 18:1-4,10; Romans 7:9). Also, Psalm 51:5 is a hyperbole (overstatement for emphasis), as are Psalm 22:9; 58:3.

CHAPTER FIVE
Spiritualism Versus Faith: Living in Christ

1. *Catholic Claim:* Confirmation is when those previously baptized receive the Holy Spirit by the laying on of the Bishop's hands.
   Bible Truth: The indwelling of the Spirit comes when a disciple is baptized (Acts 2:38; Galatians 4:6). Laying on of apostle's hands imparted the miraculous gifts of the Spirit (Acts 8:14-19).
2. *Catholic Claim:* The doctrine of penance means that a priest must forgive a person's sins.
   Bible Truth: The passages in Matthew 16:19 & 18:18 did not make the apostles into law makers; they were law enforcers. Forgiveness comes from God, but healing from our confessing to *one another* (not *priests*)—James 5:16.
3. *Catholic Claim:* Indulgences helps the deceased to get out of purgatory quicker.
   Bible Truth: There is no purgatory (Luke 16:19-31; Hebrews 9:27; once people are dead, their eternal fate is sealed.)
4. *Catholic Claim:* Jesus is sacrificed in the mass daily.
   Bible Truth: Jesus was sacrificed once for all (Hebrews 7:27).
5. *Catholic Claim:* John 6 refers to the Catholic doctrine of transubstantiation.
   Bible Truth: John 6 refers to accepting Jesus as the Son of God by accepting his teachings (compare the requirements for being raised up at the last

day— verses 39-40, 44,54). Also look at the emphasis on the words of Jesus as the means to life (verses 63, 68-69).
6. *Catholic Claim:* Practices of asceticism, such as monasticism and celibacy of the clergy, are spiritual and pleasing to God. *Bible Truth:* Such practices are neither spiritual nor helpful in avoiding sin (Colossians 2:20-23). Requiring celibacy is strictly forbidden (1 Timothy 4:1- 5); Peter was married and living with his wife (1 Corinthians 9:5).

CHAPTER SIX

A Long History of Reactions

Reaction #1 — Catholicism

1. Characterized by gradual departures from the biblical pattern in doctrine and life.
2. Eventually, this religion became a mixture of Christianity, Judaism and Paganism.
3. The ultimate excesses financially and morally led to a strong reaction among many Catholic leaders who could no longer turn their eyes away from these sins.

Reaction #2—Protestant Reformation

1. *Key figures:* Martin Luther, Huldreich Zwingli, John Calvin.
2. *Main accomplishments:* Stood up against the existing religious corruption and advocated a return to biblical authority.
3. *Weaknesses:* Did not go far enough, for more was needed than a mere reformation of the existing church.

Reaction #3—Restoration Movement

1. *Key figures:* Thomas and Alexander Campbell, Barton W. Stone, Walter Scott.
2. *Main accomplishments:* Rejection of human creeds in favor of the Bible alone. Plea was for restoration of the original church rather then reformation of an existing one. Doctrinal positives were a much more accurate understanding of baptism, and a rejection of the Calvinistic underpinnings of mainline Protestantism.
3. *Weaknesses:* Allowed the mission to become sidetracked due to a doctrinal focus at the expense of personal discipleship. Legalism became rampant, and a true understanding of biblical repentance was lost.

Reaction #4—Holiness Movement

1. *Underlying causes of this movement:* Breakdown of morals in society, and formalism and deadness of existing churches.
2. *Strengths:* Having the desire to have a meaningful personal relationship with God, to live more holy lives, and to allow the Spirit to work in their churches.
3. *Weaknesses:* Going after good *ends* by using unbiblical *means*. The doctrines regarding the miraculous gifts of the Holy Spirit are misunderstood and misapplied.

Reaction #5—Discipleship Movement (International Churches of Christ)

1. *Early contributing influences:* Chuck Lucas and the Crossroads Church of Christ in Gainesville, Florida.
2. *Strengths:* Commitment to, and insistence on, every member being a true

disciple, determined to maintain a close personal relationship with God while making other disciples; every church being totally dedicated to carrying the gospel to every nation; caring for the poor and needy in a significant way worldwide and in their own communities.

3. *Challenges:* Keeping every member zealous in his walk with God and in his evangelism; taking it much higher in financial sacrifices to support the plans for world evangelism; every church staying "on the edge," thus avoiding the spiritual plague of a lukewarm fringe. Allowing no one and nothing to slow or stop us in our world mission as God's modern-day movement.

CHAPTER SEVEN

Calvinism: The Doctrinal Basis of Protestantism

1. *Calvinistic Claim:* Every person is born guilty of Adamic sin, and in fact, is *totally* depraved.
   Bible Truth: Jesus spoke of those with "good and honest" hearts, who could thus choose to obey God (Luke 8:11-15). Cornelius had impressed God with his heart, even as a non-Christian (Acts 10:1-4). Deceivers were said to go from "bad to worse," which makes no sense if they were already totally depraved (2 Timothy 3:13).
2. *Calvinistic Claim:* Due to man's supposed total depravity, God's election of man must be *unconditional.*
   Bible Truth: God does not show favoritism, but accepts those who choose to do right (Acts 10:34-35). God does not want the wicked to die, but rather to repent (Ezekiel 33:11). The potter and clay illustration of Romans 9 does not mean that the clay has nothing to do with how it is shaped (2 Timothy 2:20-21). God calls us by the gospel (2 Thessalonians 2:13-14), and he wants all to receive this call (Mark 16:15), but we have the responsibility to accept the "clothing" offered to us as we choose to be chosen (Matthew 22:1-14).
3. *Calvinistic Claim:* The atonement was limited, hence Christ died *only* for the elect.
   Bible Truth: Jesus clearly died for everyone, although everyone will not accept him. See Luke 2:10; John 1:29; John 3:16; 2 Corinthians 5:14-15; 1 Timothy 2:5-6; Hebrews 2:9; 1 John 2:2.
4. *Calvinistic Claim:* God's grace is *irresistible* to the ones whom he has elected.
   Bible Truth: All of the choices given by God in his word would make no sense at all unless they are indeed genuine choices (Luke 9:23; Acts 2:40; Romans 2:6- 11; Hebrews 3:25; 12:25). Jesus says very pointedly that we *can* choose to do God's will (John 7:17).
5. *Calvinistic Claim:* If a person is one of the elect, he will become a Christian, and he will persevere (cannot fall away).
   Bible Truth: Hebrews is an entire book warning about this possibility (Hebrews 2:1-3; 3:7-13: 6:4-6; 10:26-31; 12:25). Compare the *will not's* in John 3:36 and John 5:24. Why would one be *reversible* and the other *irreversible*? An unbeliever can become a believer, and a believer can become an unbeliever

(Hebrews 3:12). See John 15:5-6; 1 Corinthians 9:27; Galatians 5:4; and 2 Peter 2:20-22 for similar passages.

CHAPTER EIGHT

Protestant Doctrines of Salvation

1. *Protestant Infant Baptism Doctrine:* Infant baptism takes the place of circumcision in the OT.
   Bible Truth: The passage often used to support the above claim (Colossians 2:11-12) actually teaches the opposite, for it shows personal faith of the one being baptized (impossible for an infant). In Hebrews 8:11, we find that the basic difference in entering the OT and NT covenants was that in the former, you were born and then taught, whereas in the latter, you are first taught and then born (reborn spiritually). This order now rules out infants experiencing the new birth, for they must be old enough to be taught *first.*
2. *Evangelical Adult Baptism Doctrine:* A person is saved at the point of faith and then baptized later as "an outward sign of an inward grace."
   Bible Truth: Baptism is the culminating act of becoming a Christian (Acts 2:38; Acts 22:16; Romans 6:2-4; Galatians 3:26-27; 1 Peter 3:21). Romans 10:9-10 does not teach *faith only* because calling on the name of the Lord in verse 12 includes baptism (Compare Acts 2:21 with Acts 2:37-38; then, Acts 22:16). Salvation is "in Christ" (2 Timothy 2:10), and only three passages tell us how to get "into" Christ (1 Corinthians 12:13; Romans 6:3-4; Galatians 3:26-27). The word "faith" may be used in a narrow way (John 12:42; Acts 11:21) or in a broad way (Romans 1:16; Acts 4:4). In the latter case, faith *includes* baptism (Acts 16:30-34). Further, in that broad usage, faith and obedience are used interchangeably (John 3:36; Acts 14:1-2; 19:1-3; Hebrews 3:18-19). The city of Jericho was a gift, with conditions attached (Joshua 6), and when the walls fell, it was faith that caused it. But, faith caused the walls of Jericho to fall *after* the conditions had been met (Hebrews 11:30). Faith saves us, *after* we have obeyed Jesus in baptism (Romans 6:17-18).

CHAPTER NINE

The "Mainline" Church of Christ

1. *Mainline Church of Christ:* Can only do what is specifically *authorized.* Must be "silent" —that is not authorize or allow anything—where the Bible is silent.
   Bible Truth: Can do what is not specifically forbidden. For example, the Jews established an elaborate synagogue system, which was acceptable to God. The "pattern" view of Christianity has produced legalistic attitudes, spiritual insecurity and gross division.
2. *Mainline Church of Christ:* Church autonomy is God's plan for each congregation.
   Bible Truth: Such autonomy is neither biblical nor practical, as the extremely divided state of the Mainline Church of Christ amply demonstrates. The "one

church" of Ephesians 4:4 is the same universal church in which Christ put leaders for the purpose of maturing and uniting this one church (Ephesians 4:11-16). The first century church evangelized the world through their unity and cooperation brought about by the "world Christian" concept of leaders and members. The leaders were linked together in their training and in their mission. Discipleship is a vital ingredient for this kind of success.

3. *Mainline Church of Christ:* The use of instrumental music in worship to God is sinful because only singing is mentioned in the NT.
   Bible Truth: Singing is required because it is mentioned, but playing is optional because it is not mentioned. The Jewish Christians continued to practice a number of Jewish customs, and it would be difficult to imagine that taking vows and shaving your head was acceptable, but playing music was not.
4. *Mainline Church of Christ:* Women cannot share personal testimonies or anything similar in worship assemblies; they can only sing.
   Bible Truth: The focus of 1 Timothy 2:8-15 is that women's demeanor is to be quiet (not silent), not teaching men or assuming authority over men. The women who were to remain "silent" in 1 Corinthians 14:34-35 were evidently wives of inspired speakers who were interrupting their husbands and disrupting assemblies. If "silent" applies to all women, they could not even sing in services, because the word means absolute silence. 1 Corinthians 11:3-16 shows that women prayed and prophesied in the early church during the miraculous days of the miraculous gifts. To say that our women cannot even share is to take a bold leap of opinion (not faith).

CHAPTER TEN
Pentecostalism

1. *Pentecostal Claim:* Every Christian needs spiritual gifts, especially the gift of speaking in tongues.
   Bible Truth: The purpose of the miraculous gifts was to reveal and confirm the Word (Mark 16:15-20; Hebrews 2:1-4). Now that the Word has been confirmed and written, the written accounts of miracles can produce the same faith in us that the direct miracles did in the early church (John 20:30-31). Further, the Scripture completely equips us (2 Timothy 3:16-17).
2. *Pentecostal Claim:* These miraculous gifts are available to Christians today.
   Bible Truth: The gifts of the Spirit were passed on by the laying on of the apostles' hands (Acts 6:6; 8:14-19; 19:1-7; Romans 1:11). Therefore, when the apostles died, the gifts could no longer be passed on. Besides this necessary conclusion, 1 Corinthians 13:8-10 predicted such an ending.
3. *Pentecostal Claim:* Speaking in tongues is possible for all Christians, and it is a type of ecstatic utterance.
   Bible Truth: Even in the first century, not everyone spoke in tongues (1 Corinthians 12:29-30). Those who did spoke in a foreign language which could be understood by those from that country (Acts 2:6,8,11). That is the meaning of glossa, the Greek word translated "tongue" or "language."

4. *Pentecostal Claim:* We can be baptized with the Holy Spirit today, enabling us to speak in tongues.
   Bible Truth: Baptism of the Spirit was the outpouring of the Spirit, which took place on Pentecost. It was a "once for all" event. Peter was reminded of it by the experience with Cornelius (Acts 10:44 and 46; 11:15-17) , but no one was ever commanded to be baptized with the Holy Spirit, and no individual in the NT is ever said to have received "the baptism of the Holy Spirit."
5. *Pentecostal Claim:* 1 Corinthians 14 proves that we should have spiritual gifts in the church today.
   Bible Truth: 1 Corinthians 14 regulated gifts for the time when they were available. A close examination of the passage shows that Pentecostal practice totally contradicts that chapter. For example, no one could speak in tongues unless an interpreter was present, and even then, no more than three could speak in any service, one at a time (verses 26-28).

CHAPTER ELEVEN
The Jehovah's Witnesses

1. *Jehovah's Witnesses Claim:* The Holy Spirit is simply God's active force, not a person.
   Bible Truth: The Spirit has the attributes and activities of a person. See Matthew 12:31-32; John 14:26; Acts 5:3; 7:51; 13:2; Romans 8:14, 26-27; 2 Corinthians 13:14; Ephesians 4:30; 1 Timothy 4:1.
2. *Jehovah's Witnesses Claim:* The concept of the Trinity is confusing and false.
   Bible Truth: God is one God, consisting of three distinct personalities (Matthew 1:18-23; 3:16-17; 28:19; 2 Corinthians 13:14; Ephesians 2:18, 21-22).
3. *Jehovah's Witnesses Claim:* Jesus is a created being, an archangel, and not Deity.
   Bible Truth: Jesus is eternal, a part of the triune God (Isaiah 9:6-7; Jeremiah 23:5-6; Micah 5:2; John 1:1; 20:28; Titus 2:13; 2 Peter 1:1; 1 John 5:20).
4. *Jehovah's Witnesses Claim:* Man does not have a soul, or spirit, that lives past the death of the body.
   Bible Truth: Man receives a spirit directly from God (Zechariah 12:1; Ecclesiastes 12:7; Hebrews 12:9). Our basic nature is that we are a spirit who lives in a body, not a body which happens to have a spirit. See Matthew 22:23-32; Luke 16:19-31; 23:43; Acts 9:39; Romans 14:8; 2 Corinthians 5:6-8; Philippians 1:21-23.
5. *Jehovah's Witnesses Claim:* Christ is coming back to earth to establish a literal 1,000 year kingdom.
   Bible Truth: The kingdom was set up on the Day of Pentecost as described in Acts 2. Revelation 20 is a symbolic passage showing the persecuted disciples of the first century that their cause would soon triumph over the persecutors. The symbols of this book cannot be forced into a literal interpretation. Compare Zechariah 6:12-13 with Acts 2 in order to see that Jesus is now reigning in his kingdom. The kingdom on earth is the church (Matthew 16:18-19),

and after Acts 2, it is described as a present reality (Colossians 1:13-4:11; Hebrews 12:28; Revelation 1:6). Actually, when Jesus comes, it will be to take us home with him (John 14:1-3; 1 Thessalonians 4:16-17), and to destroy the physical universe (2 Peter 3:10-12; Revelation 21:1).

6. *Jehovah's Witnesses Claim:* The 144,000 depicts a literal number of spiritual Jehovah's Witnesses who will go to heaven, leaving the rest of the Witnesses on the earth for eternity.
   Bible Truth: This number, in the contexts of Revelation 7 & 14, depicts all of the redeemed on earth who were undergoing that persecution, and who were going to be protected spiritually by God. If the Jehovah's Witnesses are going to take the number literally, then they need to make the rest of those passages literal as well. In this case, the 144,000 are all Jewish male virgins! As to the rest remaining on earth, there will be no earth on which to remain (2 Peter 3:10-12).

CHAPTER TWELVE
The Sabbath Keepers

1. *Sabbatarian Claim:* The Ten Commandments are moral commands for all times and for all covenants of God with men.
   Bible Truth: Nine of the Ten Commandments are restated in the NT, as is the principle behind the Sabbath (man is not to be a workaholic, and should set aside a special day for honoring God). However, we are not under the Ten Commandments. Romans 7:4-7 identifies the law to which we have died as the law which contained the law on coveting (Ten Commandments). Hebrews 8:7-12 says that we are under the new covenant rather than the old, and 1 Kings 8:9, 21 shows that the old covenant being discussed includes the Ten Commandments. 2 Corinthians 3 calls the covenant engraved on stones—the one which was done away in Christ, and this one can be none other than the Ten Commandments.
2. *Sabbatarian Claim:* The ceremonial law, called the Law of Moses, was ended at the cross, but the Ten Commandment moral law, called the Law of God, remains today.
   Bible Truth: No such distinction can be made biblically. God gave the Law of Moses (Ezra 7:6) and Moses gave the Law of God (2 Chronicles 34:14). The ceremonial parts of the law were said to be a part of the Law of the Lord in 2 Chronicles 31:3, and the moral parts were called the Law of Moses (Mark 7:10). Luke 2:22-23 uses the two designations interchangeably.
3. *Sabbatarian Claim:* The Sabbath observance was to be a perpetual, everlasting covenant based on Exodus 31:14-17.
   Bible Truth: This passage shows that the Sabbath was given only to that new nation as a sign between them and God. It also shows that words like "perpetual" and "everlasting" are to be qualified by the phrase "throughout your generations," a reference to the generations of the Jewish covenant (which ended at the cross). Nehemiah 9:13-14 and Ezekiel 20:12, 20 make it clear that the Sabbath law was not given until Mount Sinai.

Further, if the Sabbath keepers want to make their argument on the word "perpetual," then they will also have to accept the other "perpetual" requirements of Judaism (Exodus 29:9; 30:8, 21; Leviticus 23:41; Numbers 10:8).

4. *Sabbatarian Claim:* The seventh day of the week is the day of emphasis for the church.
   Bible Truth: Even though Jesus observed the Sabbath since he was born and died under the Law of Moses (Galatians 4:4), and the early preachers went into Jewish synagogues on the Sabbath in order to preach to the Jews, the first day of the week was clearly established as the day of emphasis in the early church. Jesus arose on the first day of the week (Mark 16:1-9), he appeared to his disciples on two different first days (John 20:19, 26), and the church was established on the first day of the week (Acts 2). The early disciples observed the first day as their day of assembly (Acts 20:7; 1 Corinthians 16:2).
5. *Sabbatarian Claim:* OT food laws are designed to promote good health, and they should be kept in the new covenant.
   Bible Truth: Jesus made all foods clean (Mark 7:17-19), nothing is to be rejected (1 Timothy 4:1-5), God can accept the man who chooses to eat everything, and so must other disciples (Romans 14:3); and finally, we should refuse to let anyone judge us by what we eat or drink, because these things have absolutely nothing to do with spirituality (Colossians 2:16-23).

CHAPTER THIRTEEN
The Mormons

1. *Mormonism Claim:* A number of Gods exist, and they have flesh and bones.
   Bible Truth: There is only one God, and he is spirit (Mark 12:29; Ephesians 4:6; John 4:24; Luke 24:39).
2. *Mormonism Claim:* Jesus was begotten by the Father through literal intercourse.
   Bible Truth: Jesus was begotten by the Holy Spirit through a virgin mother (Matthew 1:18-23).
3. *Mormonism Claim:* In spite of some writings which are accurate, other Mormon writings talk about God being progressive in his knowledge and power.
   Bible Truth: God is perfect and cannot change in his nature, nor can Jesus (Malachi 3:6; Hebrews 13:8).
4. *Mormonism Claim:* Jesus was married to several women and had children by them.
   Bible Truth: The only wife that Jesus has ever had is the church (2 Corinthians 11:2; Ephesians 5:25-32).
5. *Mormonism Claim:* The Book of Mormon teaches that three days of darkness occurred at Christ's crucifixion (Helaman 14:20). Alma 7:10 has Jesus being born in Jerusalem. Mosiah 18:17 speaks of the establishment of the Church of Christ in 147 BC, and Alma 46:15 says that people were called Christians (in at least 73 BC).
   Bible Truth: Three hours of darkness at the cross (Matthew 27:45); Jesus born in Bethlehem (Matthew 2:1); the establishment of the church and the first use of the name "Christian" came in the first century A.D. (Matthew 16:18; Acts 11:26).

6. *Mormonism Claim:* The spirits of humans are eternal.
   Bible Truth: Man was created totally in the beginning (Genesis 1:26-27), and our spirits are now created and placed in our physical bodies (Zechariah 12:1; Ecclesiastes 12:7). Only God is immortal (1 Timothy 6:15-16).
7. *Mormonism Claim:* Living humans can be baptized for the benefit of dead humans.
   Bible Truth: After death, no second chance (Luke 16:19-31; 2 Corinthians 5:10; Hebrews 9:27). Also, biblical baptism is always based on the personal faith and repentance of the one being baptized.
8. *Mormonism Claim:* Both Aaronic and Melchizedek priesthoods were given to them by God.
   Bible Truth: The Melchizedek priesthood is occupied by Jesus alone, and the Aaronic priesthood was a part of the old covenant which has been done away in Christ (Hebrews 7:11-12). Now, all Christians are priests (1 Peter 2:9).
9. *Mormonism Claim:* The Mormon Church has a continuing line of prophets who reveal and interpret the will of God.
   Bible Truth: Prophecy ended with the death of the first century apostles (Acts 8:9-18; 1 Corinthians 13:8-10). The apostles received all truth in the first century, and through inspiration delivered it to us (John 14:25-26; 16:13; Ephesians 3:2-5). Finally, the NT was complete and gives man all that he needs to please God (2 Timothy 3:16-17; 2 Peter 1:3; Jude 3).

PART TWO

·Resources·

The Crucifixion of Jesus

"The Passion of Christ from a Medical Point of View"

C. Truman Davis, M.D., M.S.
Reprinted with permission from *Arizona Medicine,* March 1965

In this paper, I shall discuss some of the physical aspects of the passion, or suffering, of Jesus Christ. We shall follow Him from Gethsemane, through His trial, His scourging, His path along the Via Dolorosa, to His last dying hours on the cross....

This led me first to a study of the practice of crucifixion itself; that is, the torture and execution of a person by fixation to a cross. Apparently, the first known practice of crucifixion was by the Persians. Alexander and his generals brought it back to the Mediterranean world - to Egypt and Carthage. The Romans apparently learned the practice from the Carthaginians and (as with almost everything the Romans did) rapidly developed a very high degree of efficiency and skill in carrying it out. A number of Roman authors (Livy, Cicero, Tacitys) comment on it. Several innovations and modifications are described in the ancient literature; I'll mention only a few which may have some bearing here. The upright portion of the cross (or stipes) could have the cross-arm (or patibulum) attached two or three feet below its top - this is what we commonly think of today as the classical form of the cross (the one which we have later named the Latin cross); however, the common form used in Our Lord's day was the Tau cross (shaped like the Greek letter Tau or like our T). In this cross the patibulum was placed in a notch at the top of the stipes. There is fairly overwhelming archeological evidence that it was on this type of cross that Jesus was crucified.

The upright post, or stipes, was generally permanently fixed in the ground at the site of execution and the condemned man was forced to carry the patibulum, apparently weighing about 110 pounds, from the prison to the place of execution. Without any historical or biblical proof, medieval and Renaissance painters have given us our picture of Christ carrying the entire cross. Many of these painters and most of the sculptors of crucifixes today show the nails through the palms. Roman historical accounts and experimental work have shown that the nails were driven between the small bones of the wrists and not through the palms. Nails driven through the palms will strip out between the fingers when they support the weight of a human body. The misconception may have come about through a misunderstanding of Jesus' words to Thomas, *"Observe my hands."* Anatomists, both modern and ancient, have always considered the wrists as part of the hand.

A titulus, or small sign, stating the victim's crime was usually carried at the front of the processions and later nailed to the cross above the head. This sign with its staff nailed to the top of the cross would have given it somewhat the characteristic form of the Latin cross.

Gethsemane

The physical passion of the Christ begins in Gethsemane. Of the many aspects of this initial suffering, I shall only discuss the one of physiological interest; the bloody sweat. It is interesting that the physician of the group, St. Luke, is the only one to mention this. He says, *"And being in agony, He prayed the longer. And his sweat became as drops of blood, trickling down upon the ground."*

Every attempt imaginable has been used by modern scholars to explain away this phrase, apparently under the mistaken impression that this just doesn't happen.

A great deal of effort could be saved by consulting the medical literature. Though very rare, the phenomenon of Hematidrosis or bloody sweat, is well documented. Under great emotional stress, tiny capillaries in the sweat glands can break, thus mixing blood with sweat. This process alone could have produced marked weakness and possible shock.

We shall move rapidly through the betrayal and arrest; I must stress that important portions of the passion story are missing from this account. This may be frustrating to you, but in order to adhere to our purpose of discussing only the purely physical aspects of the Passion, this is necessary. After the arrest in the middle of the night, Jesus was brought before the Sanhedrin and Caiaphas, the High Priest; it is here that the first physical trauma as inflicted. A soldier struck Jesus across the face for remaining silent when questioned by Caiaphas. The palace guards then blindfolded Him and mockingly taunted Him to identify them as they each passed by, spat on Him, and struck Him in the face.

Before Pilate

In the morning, Jesus, battered and bruised, dehydrated, and exhausted from a sleepless night, is taken across Jerusalem to the Praetorium of the Fortress Antonia, the seat of government of the Procurator of Judea, Pontius Pilate. You are, of course, familiar with Pilate's action in attempting to pass responsibility to Herod Antipas, the Tetrarch of Judea. Jesus apparently suffered no physical mistreatment at the hands of Herod and was returned to Pilate.

It was then, in response to the cries of the mob, that Pilate ordered Bar-Abbas released and condemned Jesus to scourging and crucifixion. There is much disagreement among authorities about scourging as a prelude to crucifixion. Most Roman writers from this period do not associate the two. Many scholars believe that Pilate originally ordered Jesus scourged as his full punishment and that the death sentence by crucifixion came only in response to the taunt by the mob that the Procurator was not properly defending Caesar against this pretender who claimed to be the King of the Jews.

The Scourging

Preparations for the scourging are carried out. The prisoner is stripped of His clothing and His hands tied to a post above His head. It is doubtful whether the Romans made any attempt to follow the Jewish law in this matter of scourging. The Jews had an ancient law prohibiting more than forty lashes. The Pharisees, always making sure that the law was strictly kept, insisted that only thirty-nine lashes be given. (In case of miscount, they were sure of remaining within the law.) The Roman legionnaire steps forward with the flagrum (or flagellum) in his hand. This is a short whip consisting of several heavy, leather thongs with two small balls of lead attached near the ends of each.

The heavy whip is brought down with full force again and again across Jesus' shoulders, back and legs. At first the heavy thongs cut through the skin only. Then, as the blows continue, they cut deeper into the subcutaneous tissues, producing first an oozing of blood from the capillaries and veins of the skin, and finally spurting arterial bleeding from vessels in the underlying muscles. The small balls of lead first produce large, deep bruises which are broken open by subsequent blows. Finally the skin of the back is hanging in long ribbons and the entire area is an unrecognizable mass of torn, bleeding tissue. When it is determined by the centurion in charge that the prisoner is near death, the beating is finally stopped.

The half-fainting Jesus is then untied and allowed to slump to the stone pavement, wet with His own blood. The Roman soldiers see a great joke in this provincial Jew claiming to be a king. They throw a robe across His shoulders and place a stick in His hand for a scepter. They still need a crown to make their travesty complete. A small bundle of flexible branches covered with long thorns (commonly used for firewood) are plaited into the shape of a crown and this is pressed into His scalp. Again there is copious bleeding (the scalp being one of the most vascular areas of the body). After mocking Him and striking Him across the face, the soldiers take the stick from His hand and strike Him across the head, driving the thorns deeper into His scalp. Finally, they tire of their sadistic sport and the robe is torn from His back. This had already become adherent to the clots of blood and serum in the wounds, and its removal, just as in the careless removal of a surgical bandage, causes excruciating pain...almost as though He were again being whipped - and the wounds again begin to bleed.

In deference to Jewish custom, the Romans return His garments. The heavy patibulum of the cross is tied across His shoulders and the procession of the condemned Christ, two thieves and the execution detail of the Roman soldiers, headed by a centurion, begins it slow journey along the Via Dolorosa. In spite of His efforts to walk erect, the weight of the heavy wooden cross together with the shock produced by copious blood loss, is too much. He stumbles and falls. The rough wood of the beam gouges into the lacerated skin and muscles of the shoulders. He tries to rise, but human muscles have been pushed beyond their endurance. The centurion, anxious to get on with the crucifixion, selects a stalwart North African onlooker, Simon of Cyrene, to carry the cross. Jesus follows, still bleeding and sweating the cold, clammy sweat of shock. The 650-yard journey from the fortress Antonia to Golgotha is finally completed. The prisoner is again stripped of His clothes - except for a loin cloth which is allowed the Jews.

The Crucifixion

The crucifixion begins, Jesus is offered wine mixed with Myrrh, a mild analgesic mixture. He refuses to drink. Simon is ordered to place the cross on the ground and Jesus is quickly thrown backward with His shoulders against the wood. The legionnaire feels for the depression at the front of the wrist. He drives a heavy, square, wrought-iron nail through the wrist and deep into the wood. Quickly, he moves to the other side and repeats the action, being careful not to pull the arms too tightly, but to allow some flexibility and movement. The patibulum is then lifted in place at the top of the stipes and the titulus reading *"Jesus of Nazareth, King of the Jews"* is nailed in place.

The left foot is pressed backward against the right foot, and with both feet extended, toes down, a nail is driven through the arch of each, leaving the knees moderately flexed. The victim is now crucified. As He slowly sags down with more weight on the nails in the wrists, excruciating, fiery pain shoots along the fingers and up the arms to explode in the brain - the nails in the wrists are putting pressure on the median nerves. As He pushes Himself upward to avoid this wrenching torment, He places His full weight on the nail through His feet. Again there is the searing agony of the tearing through the nerves between the metatarsal bones of the feet.

At this point, another phenomenon occurs. As the arms fatigue, great waves of cramps sweep over the muscles, knotting them in deep, relentless, throbbing pain. With these cramps comes the inability to push Himself upward. Hanging by His arms, the pectoral muscles are paralyzed and the intercostal muscles are unable to act. Air can be drawn into the lungs, but cannot be exhaled. Jesus fights to raise Himself in order to get even one short breath. Finally carbon dioxide builds up in the lungs and in the blood stream and the cramps partially subside. Spasmodically, He is able to push Himself upward to exhale and bring in the life-giving oxygen. It was undoubtedly during these periods that He uttered the seven short sentences which are recorded:

The first, looking down at the Roman soldiers throwing dice for His seamless garment, *"Father, forgive them for they know not what they do."*

The second, to the penitent thief, *"Today thou shalt be with me in Paradise."*

The third, looking down at the terrified, grief stricken, adolescent John, (the beloved Apostle), He said, *"Behold thy mother,"* and looking to Mary, His mother, *"Woman, behold thy son."*

The fourth cry is from the beginning of the 22nd Psalm, *"My God, my God, why hast thou forsaken me?"*

Hours of this limitless pain, cycles of twisting joint-rending cramps, intermittent partial asphyxiation, searing pain as tissue is torn from His lacerated back as He moves up and down against the rough timber. Then another agony begins. A deep, crushing pain deep in the chest as the pericardium slowly fills with serum and begins to compress the heart.

Let us remember again the 22nd Psalm (the 14th verse), *"I am poured out like water, and all my bones are out of joint; my heart is like wax, it is melted in the midst of my bowels."* It is now almost over - the loss of tissue fluids has reached a critical level - the compressed heart is struggling to pump heavy, thick, sluggish blood into the tissue - the tortured lungs are making a frantic effort to draw in small gulps of air. The markedly dehydrated tissues send their flood of stimuli to the brain.

Jesus gasps His fifth cry, *"I thirst."*

Let us remember another verse from the prophetic 22nd Psalm: *"My strength is dried up like a potsherd, and my tongue cleaveth to my jaws; and thou has brought me into the dust of death."*

A sponge soaked in Posca, the cheap, sour wine which is the staple drink of the Roman legionnaires, is lifted to His lips. He apparently does not take any of the liquid. The body of Jesus is now in extremis, and He can feel the chill of death creeping through His tissues. This realization brings out His sixth words - possibly little more than a tortured whisper.

"It is finished."

His mission of atonement has been completed. Finally He can allow his body to die.

With one last surge of strength, he once again presses His torn feet against the nail, straightens His legs, takes a deeper breath, and utters His seventh and last cry, *"Father into thy hands I commit my spirit."*

The rest you know. In order that the Sabbath not be profaned, the Jews asked that the condemned men be dispatched and removed from the crosses. The common method of ending a crucifixion was by cruxifracture, the breaking of the bones of the legs. This prevents the victim from pushing himself upward; the tension could not be relieved from the muscles of the chest, and rapid suffocation occurred. The legs of the two thieves were broken, but when they came to Jesus they saw that this was unnecessary, thus fulfilling the scripture, *"not one bone shall be broken."*

Apparently to make doubly sure of death, the legionnaire drove his lance through the fifth interspace between the ribs, upward through the pericardium and into the heart. The 34th verse of the 19th chapter of the Gospel according to John: *"And immediately there came out blood and water."* Thus there was an escape of watery fluid from the sac surrounding the heart and blood from the interior of the heart. We, therefore, have rather conclusive postmortem evidence that Our Lord died, not the usual crucifixion death by suffocation, but of heart failure due to shock and constriction of the heart by fluid in the pericardium.

Thus we have seen a glimpse of the epitome of evil which man can exhibit toward man - and toward God. This is not a pretty sight and is apt to leave us despondent and depressed. How grateful we can be that we have a sequel: A glimpse of the infinite mercy of God toward man - the miracle of the atonement and the expectation of Easter morning!

Church History in Miniature

by Tom Jones and Roger Lamb

Originally titled

"You Might Be Fighting God"

Reprinted with permission from *Discipleship Magazine*, Spring 1991

A guide to understanding what has happened in almost 2000 years of church history—and exciting news of what God is doing in our day.

> *"Let them go! For if their purpose or activity is of human origin, it will fail. But if it is from God, you will not be able to stop these men; you will only find yourselves fighting against God."*
>
> GAMALIEL, RENOWNED JEWISH LEADER, SPEAKING TO THE SANHEDRIN ABOUT THE DISCIPLES OF JESUS (ACTS 5:38-39)

In reality, there was good reason for Gamaliel to issue this warning to his fellow Jews of the first century. After God delivered his Old Testament people from their slavery in Egypt, one could almost describe the history of the Jews as the history of a people fighting God. There were exceptions, of course. There were individuals here and there who loved God and wanted to live for him. There were times when great leaders moved the people as a whole to acts of faith and obedience, but the overall trend was in another direction. From the time of the Exodus to the time of Jesus, those who were the objects of God's affection were often in rebellion against his plans for their lives.

Stephen, that Spirit-filled Hellenistic Jew, preaching to the Jewish ruling counsel after the death of Jesus, proclaimed that Jewish history was the story of their rejection of God. He concluded powerfully with these words:

> *"You stiff-necked people, with uncircumcised hearts and ears! You are just like your fathers: You always resist the Holy Spirit! Was there ever a prophet your fathers did not persecute? They even killed those who predicted the coming of the Righteous One. And now you have betrayed and murdered him" (Acts 7:51-52).*

For hundreds of years, God had been trying to love them and lead them, but for most of those years they had been fighting God.

Sadly, the history of Christianity, particularly after the first century, has often been a repeat of the Old Testament story. The church of Jesus began in a great way and had great impact, but eventually came adrift from the exciting truths that turned the world upside down. Yes, there have been heroic personalities. There have been those with great courage who from time to time rose up and insisted on returning to the Scriptures. There have been people consumed with the mission of Jesus, but there has been much tragic confusion and division because, in reality, many were fighting God and not submitting to him.

Obviously a short article has great limitations in attempting to describe something as complex as more than 1900 years of church history, but many people do not have even a rudimentary understanding of how we got from the dynamic first-century church to the divided religious world of today. Our goal is to give you the basic outline.

I. 100-312 A.D.—Growth and Departures

The first-century church experienced remarkable growth. Starting in a lightly regarded place in the expansive Roman Empire, within 30 years it had established strong beachheads in most of the great population centers and in many places in between. From a human point of view, the church should not have enjoyed such success, but God had chosen the right time to send his son (Galatians 4:4), the gospel was the power of God and the church was indwelt by the Holy Spirit. By the time Paul wrote the letter to the Colossians, he could say that the gospel had "been proclaimed to every creature under heaven" (Colossians 1:23).

As the church moved on into the second and third centuries growth continued, even as the church was frequently persecuted. However, with the passing of the apostles, growth was accompanied by false doctrines. Consider three examples:

1. Different teachings grew up which tried to rob Jesus of his identity as the one and only true son of God. Some began explaining Jesus to be a man who was like God, and strong objection was made to his being deity. Another group, the Gnostics, taught that Jesus was deity but not really a man in the flesh. The Apostle Paul had corrected the first view, "For in Christ all the fullness of the Deity lives in bodily form" (Colossians 2:9). The Apostle John had addressed the Gnostics in 1 John, "Every Spirit that acknowledges that Jesus Christ has come in the flesh is from God, but every spirit that does not acknowledge Jesus is not from God" (1 John 4:34). Throughout history, groups would rise up and disappear, claiming these same false teachings. In our day there are those ranging from the Universalists to the Jehovah's Witnesses and Mormons.
2. The New Testament had taught that baptism by immersion was for the forgiveness of sins (Acts 2:38; Romans 6:3-7) but it was equally clear that people who sinned after baptism could be forgiven. 1 John 1 and 2 teach that everyone will need such forgiveness. The second and third century churches clearly taught that baptism brought forgiveness, but they eventually taught that there were three sins that the church could never forgive after baptism, even though they might be forgiven by God (a strange doctrine indeed!). These three were murder, sexual immorality and the denial of the faith.
3. During the two centuries following the apostles, persecutions of the church came and went. One of the worst came around 250 A.D. with believers being threatened, then tortured until they renounced their faith, and many did. While some survived, still confessing their faith, others were martyred. After the persecutions, Cyprian, the Bishop of Carthage, devised a plan of penance (works) to restore those who had denied their faith,

> making it more complicated for those who were guilty of the worst violations. Certainly, no such plan can be found in the New Testament where forgiveness is ever earned.

There is no doubt that the church in the first three centuries was under much stress and pressure and that there were some heroic personalities who held to Jesus, but we can see fairly early a trend toward resolving matters with human logic, not with a careful study of Scripture. Such a trend laid the basis for the coming of the Catholic Church.

II 312-600 A.D.—The State Adopts the Church

The changing attitude of the state toward the church was in many ways the most significant development during this period. After enduring persecution from the government for most of its history, the church first found itself in a position of being tolerated, then being granted more privileges and finally being officially embraced by the Roman government (395 A.D.). So complete was the relationship between church and state, that the emperor himself became the initiator of the ecumenical councils, in which the bishops came together to define and agree on doctrine. A worse development may not have been possible. When Christianity is tied to governments, the biblical challenge to the world always suffers.

During this period the hierarchy of the church solidified and became a kingdom of this world. Emphasis shifted from following Jesus to preserving the structure and position of the church. The church drifted farther from its original passion and commission to save souls, and authority was seen coming from the decisions of the priesthood and bishops instead of from the Bible. For the first time we see the papacy as a widely accepted institution. Infant baptism by pouring and then sprinkling replaced the original immersion of committed adult believers in the first century.

Augustine became the most influential theologian of this time as he laid down doctrinal roots for the teachings of original sin, celibacy and the elevation of church tradition to be equal with Scripture: "I should not believe the Gospel unless I were moved to do so by the authority of the Catholic Church." He is often referred to as the "father of the (Catholic) church."

By 600 A.D. all the essential ingredients were in place for almost a 1000 years of virtually unchallenged Catholicism. The "presbyters" (elders) of the New Testament (who were to be the husbands of one wife) had now been transformed into parish priests (who could never marry), the Lord's Supper was now a sacrament that could only be administered by the priests, the worship of Mary was well under way and the Bishop of Rome as Pope was almost universally accepted. History, politics and tradition were the greatest influences and Scripture was mostly lost in the shuffle.

600-1500—Catholicism in Full Bloom

Gregory the Great, the first pope of this period was a man of high morals who stressed spiritual qualities and reacted negatively to the title of universal bishop, preferring to be called instead "the servant of servants." However, his teachings often included the superstitions, and even pagan ideas, of the masses that were being meshed together with biblical ideas. Under his leadership anti-Scriptural ideas such as penance and purgatory were further developed and strengthened.

After Gregory, the papacy began a moral descent reaching bottom during the tenth and eleventh centuries. Popes of the latter period were found to be guilty of all kinds of incredible excesses and immorality causing the papacy to lose credibility. Eventually there were reform movements that brought the popes back into greater influence, but various efforts from outside the hierarchy to call people back to the simplicity of the Bible were squelched. The Bible had become the property of the educated clergy and was considered "too difficult" and "too holy" for the common masses. Eventually the reading of Scripture by anyone other than priests was officially condemned. Also during this time hundreds of years and lives were spent in building massive cathedrals that were now viewed to be "God's house," straying from the liberating New Testament concept of all disciples apart from buildings being a temple of the Holy Spirit. The church in the minds of most became the hierarchy and the building.

During this period, after years of simmering problems, the final break between the Eastern (or Orthodox) Church and the Western (or Roman Catholic) Church took place, with the patriarch and the pope both excommunicating the other (ca. 1050 A.D.). Significant is the fact that neither group was making any real appeal to Scripture to back their dogmas.

Occupying much attention during at least two hundred years of this period were the much talked about Crusades in which soldiers fought in the name of Christ to take the Holy Land away from the Muslims. There was even a tragic Children's Crusade that brought death to many children who left their homes in 1212 to go fight the unbelievers, believing God would bless those with purer hearts. This is a far cry from Jesus' declaration, "my kingdom is not of this world."

Monasticism and asceticism under the leadership of such men as Francis of Assisi became popular during this period. Whole movements of people mistakenly thought the only way to be truly holy was to seclude themselves from the world and to follow severe regimens of self-deprivation (Colossians 2:16-23). More and more men and women were taught that salvation was a matter of receiving the right sacraments, doing the right acts of penance, learning to use all the right symbols (e.g. the sign of the cross) and venerating the right objects (e.g. statues of Mary or relics from the past)—things noticeably absent in the Scriptures.

IV. 1500-1700—Rediscovering the Bible: The Protestant Reformation

On October 31, 1517, the Spirit of God moved a thirty-four year-old German priest named Martin Luther, to post 95 theses on the castle door at Wittenburg University, and what would be known as the Protestant Reformation was underway. Preceded by courageous but persecuted thinkers like John Wyclif (in England) and John Hus (in Bohemia) and inspired by studies in Romans and Galatians, Luther decided he could no longer be silent in the face of a religious system that had replaced the commands of God with the traditions of men. The center of his message was (1) justification by faith (in opposition to the Catholic idea of justification by works) and (2) the belief that Scripture alone (and not the edicts of popes and councils) is the authoritative standard. In *The Babylonian Captivity of the Church* he challenged so much that had become a part of traditional Roman Catholicism (including the sacraments, the priesthood and the papacy). In 1521, after saying his conscience was held captive by the word of God, he was expelled from the Catholic Church by Pope Leo X. Eventually new churches were set up where one found missing the office of bishop, the mass, the priesthood, the restrictions on marriage, and the statues. In their place was an emphasis on teaching and preaching the word of God.

The steps Luther took against an intimidating system must be appreciated. His was a major move away from an apostate church. Sadly, Luther's reforms of the church did not lead to discipling relationships nor to reform of his own character. He himself wrote that he was often lacking in self-control and could be rude or even coarse in his dealings with people. What resulted from his reforms was not a full return to biblical practice but a denomination named for him (contrary to the teachings of 1 Corinthians 1:12).

Contemporary with Luther were other reformers such as Ulrich Zwingli who led much of Switzerland in a revolt against Catholicism and John Calvin, a brilliant young scholar from France. In 1536 Calvin published his *Institutes of the Christian Religion* which became known as the landmark work of the reformation. From Calvin came the "reformed tradition" which later included the Dutch Reform Church, the Church of Scotland, Presbyterians and Baptists, unfortunately emphasizing his five major doctrines, summarized with the TULIP acrostic. They were: (1) total depravity of man, (2) unconditional forgiveness by God, (3) limited atonement (i.e. Jesus did not die for everyone), (4) irresistible grace (i.e. those elected to be saved cannot resist the grace of God, and (5) perseverance of the saints (more popularly presented as "once saved, always saved").

Those of us in the modern multiplying ministries movement may find our closest kinship in the Reformation in that group known as the Anabaptists (a name given by their opponents who despised the idea that they taught that you should be baptized again). Considered "radicals" and "fanatics" even by reformers like Luther and Calvin, this group sought a more thorough return to New Testament Christianity. Speaking plainly about "discipleship," they rejected the idea of infant baptism, insisting that every person who follows Jesus must make his own decision to be baptized based on his own faith and conviction. They insisted on being the very kind of church described in the Bible and that church was not an institution that made alliances with the state but was a family of believers who were sent by God to be salt and light in a sick and dying world. In perhaps the greatest move toward a biblical church, disciples were expected to help one another actually obey all the teachings of Jesus. Protestantism, in their view, had not gone nearly far enough. As a result these people were severely condemned by the likes of Luther, Calvin and Zwingli, and terribly persecuted by the members of the mainstream Reformation as the reformers had been persecuted. Those caught "rebaptizing" were officially executed by drowning.

The Reformation in England was a very different sort of story from that on the continent. It was not biblical conviction but pure political expediency that lead Henry VIII to renounce the authority of the pope and transform the Catholic Church in England into the Church of England. The king had wanted the pope to annul his marriage so that he would be free to marry the younger Anne Boleyn. When the pope refused, Henry declared the Church of England to be a separate organization and secured from it the permission to remarry. He was not really interested in changing any doctrines, and for half a century the Church of England (or Anglican Church) would swing back and forth sometimes in the direction of Protestantism and sometimes in the direction of Catholicism but there was never any real passion for biblical Christianity.

Catholicism obviously suffered losses during the Reformation period, but eventually mounted a counter-reformation and an internal reform movement of its own in an attempt to blunt the effect of the Protestants. Led by such men as Ignatius Loyola they attempted to revive spiritual concerns and interest in converting the pagans. However, at the famous Council of Trent they specifically rejected the Reformation doctrines, insisting that Luther's idea of "Scripture alone" was false and reaffirming their belief in the authority of the pope and the bishops. Meanwhile, since Gutenburg's invention of the printing press in 1455, the Bible had been translated into the common language of the people and spread among the common man fueling the Reformation and leading to the modern day.

V. 1700-Present—A House Divided: The Dominance of Denominationalism and Loss of Faith

Two major developments characterize the last 300 years of "modern Christianity." The first is loss of faith. As the western world grew more educated, industrialized, mechanized and now digitized, the cultures where Christianity was dominant became very impressed with what man could do. God was relegated to an irrelevant slice of life or molded into any shape that would serve man. Science and progress puffed up human ego. God was now measured by man's scientific method instead of men being measured by God's word and spirit. The result was an incredible faith in scientific theory and unscrupulous doubt in the Bible. The major universities once founded on verbalized allegiance to God now scoff at his very existence. Seminaries still produce far more doubt than faith.

The second major development was "denominationalism." Religious people had seen the number of groups that came out of the Reformation and gave up on the ideal of being one body in Christ as Jesus himself prayed for us to do (John 17). They decided to think of each group as a part of the larger body of Christ even if the groups were disunited in conviction, thought and practice.

Most people recognized that this was not the ideal way for the church of Christ to function, but it was felt that it was a great improvement on the literal warfare that had characterized religious disagreements for many years. The result has been that for 300 years or more denominations have been an accepted part of the religious landscape, with split after split after split creating an incredible proliferation of groups all wearing different names, from the mainstream Baptist, Methodist and Presbyterian to the smaller splinters like the Fire Baptized Holiness Church of God of the Americas.

Early in the nineteenth century in the United States there were those who sought another path. Believing denominationalism was against the spirit of unity found in the New Testament, leaders like Barton Stone and Thomas and Alexander Campbell (all from Presbyterian roots) and James O'Kelley (from the Methodist tradition), called for an effort to unite the sects. Their unity efforts eventually caused them to seek "a restoration of the New Testament church" which led to a rediscovery of certain biblical doctrines such as adult immersion for the forgiveness of sins. This movement which eventually produced such groups known as the Disciples of Christ, the Christian Church, and the Churches of Christ was for over a century the fastest growing indigenous religious movement in the United States. However, power struggles, the Civil War and quarreling over words led this unity movement into its own divisions and either legalistic viewpoints or abandonment of the restoration idea. Later these churches would suffer from a consuming materialism and loss of evangelistic zeal and purpose and the growth became a decline. However, within this movement would be found the seeds of our own multiplying ministries movement. From a small beginning in churches of Christ came a renewed vision to truly be the New Testament church with its central goal of carrying out The Great Commission.

Another very interesting development in the United States was the Student Volunteer Movement for Foreign Missions conceived by Dwight L. Moody at Northfield, Massachusetts in 1886. This movement rapidly spread throughout the campuses with a call for students to commit their lives to "the evangelization of this world in this generation." Campus ministries were started at prestigious schools that were founded as religious institutions but had become hostile to Christianity. After World War 1, the Student Volunteer Movement declined, but it is estimated that it moved 20,000 students to become missionaries. This was the forerunner of InterVarsity Christian Fellowship, Campus Crusade for Christ and the Navigators who emerged in the 1940s and '50s.

VI. The Restoration of New Testament Discipleship in Our Day

The '60s and '70s were troubled times in the United States. The dreamers of the country, John and Bobby Kennedy and Martin Luther King, were assassinated. The sexual revolution, Vietnam and Watergate ate away the fabric of moral conviction and self-respect in American society. Meanwhile, God was raising up people who knew Jesus was the only real way to live. Disheartened with empty secular materialism, bankrupt religious ritual, tradition and prejudice, many in the churches of Christ searched the Scriptures for a renewed vision of what Jesus' church should be. Suddenly the '70s blossomed with soul winning workshops, schools of preaching, and bus ministries. This period also saw unrest on the U.S. campuses give birth to dynamic campus ministries. Their emphasis on Jesus and the Bible captured the imagination of disillusioned youth across the nation. However, when put to the test of criticism, purity, humility and conviction, these various efforts failed Jesus' call for unity and commitment.

It was at this moment that God raised up Kip and Elena McKean to start a movement that has spread around the world to every major city in only 12 years. Beginning in 1979 with a small church of 30 in Boston, Massachusetts, God grew the Boston Church of Christ to a Sunday attendance approaching 5,000 at the famed Boston Garden, the largest church ever to meet in skeptical New England. Kip's powerful, distinctive message was simply calling people back to the original message of Jesus: That you must be a disciple of Jesus to have a relationship with God and therefore, to be a Christian, and that Christ's church is made up of disciples only. Thousands of marriages and broken homes have been healed. People enslaved by alcohol, drugs, abuse and violence have been transformed as they have totally committed their lives to following Jesus. Hypocrites have repented and hatred, jealousy, greed and immorality have been replaced with love, peace, patience and joy with a purpose. Disciples are multiplying around the globe every day without advertising, televangelism and church buildings—they just preach the Word.

The following is McKean's own account of the history of the multiplying ministries (sometimes referred to as the Boston Movement) from his "Ten-year Report" published in the *Boston Bulletin* (June 11, 1989):

> Exciting as these accounts are, the real impact of the multiplication of disciple-making began when the leadership of the Boston church decided to plant churches instead of sending our newly trained young ministers into existing congregations. In the summer of 1982, Chicago and London were planted. Shortly thereafter, the Lord put on my heart (Nehemiah 2:12) a plan to evangelize the world. By starting churches in the key cities of the world, these churches through multiplication would in time influence not just their cities, but their nation and all nations around them. These churches were called "pillar churches" for a world brotherhood was envisioned to be built on their foundation.
>
> In late 1986, it was decided to call to repentance both "mainline" and "campus ministry" churches that were willing to pay the price to multiply disciples. First we asked the interested churches' lead ministers to move to Boston to be discipled. They were then replaced with Boston-trained evangelists. During the initial weeks of this changeover, each member was called to either renew their commitment at baptism to be a disciple of Jesus, to be baptized as a disciple, or to leave. After these changes, these churches grew equally as rapidly as our plantings, for in fact there was now no difference. Each church would be comprised solely of disciples. The efforts were called "reconstructions" after the rebuilding of the wall in Jerusalem in the book of Nehemiah. Our first ones were Kingston, San Francisco and San Diego. Of great significance at this same time, London reconstructed Sydney, and Chicago reconstructed seven churches in the midwestern United States.
>
> In the many churches where there was no desire for help, an obligation to God was felt to call out the true disciples and ask them to move to the Boston churches, preferably called "multiplying ministry churches." Thus we went about gleaning the remnant into what was clearly now a movement of God. In these past ten years, the Spirit has sent disciples out from Boston to all six populated continents of the world — 29 plantings and reconstructions, 23 third-generation churches, and our first fourth-generation church—Melbourne! *[Editor's note: Spring, 1997; there are now 285 churches around the world.]*
>
> Through these past ten years there has been a constant wrestling with God through the Scriptures. As more and more churches were planted and built, the Boston leadership, as well as the couples sent out from here, found so many traditions in our backgrounds. True restoration occurred as first-century Bible doc-

trines were once more crystallized such as: baptizing only people who have made the decision to be disciples (Matthew 28:19); one church, one city (Revelation 2-3); house churches (Acts 20:20); revival of prayer and fasting (Acts 13:3); the role and power of the Holy Spirit (Romans 8); training of evangelists (Mark 3:13-14); the role of evangelists and elders (Acts 20); brotherhood, not autonomy (Ephesians 4:4); and simply believing that we are the Kingdom of God (Colossians 1:13). Perhaps one of the greatest blessings of restoration has come from Pat Gempel and Elena McKean—leadership and the role of women (Titus 2:3-5). Another immediately gratifying restoration has been in marriage and the family (Ephesians 5.22-6:4). There has never been a divorce from a marriage in the Boston church! Also the call from Douglas Arthur and the example of the London church came to all the churches to "remember the poor." Another inspiration for the movement was to come from Steve Johnson and the New York congregation—music! With every movement, secular or spiritual, music written at that hour becomes its heartbeat. Steve penned what must be considered the anthem of the movement, "Upside Down!"

The previous article documented the movement of God until June 1989 when Kip resigned the pulpit to become missions evangelist. In this role he could plant and strengthen new churches as Paul had done in the first century. The wisdom of this decision was soon confirmed as two churches that he ministered to immediately had an incredible impact: Manila, Philippines, and Los Angeles, California. Utilizing all that God had been showing over the previous years, these churches both baptized over 400 in their first year of existence, exciting everyone in the Kingdom and raising the hope and vision for the future.

Before this in 1988, after much prayer, fasting and study of the Word, a decision had been made to allow greater multiplication of the churches. Kip selected nine couples for he and Elena to focus on and gave them each a charge to lead the evangelization of their area of the world. He called them "world sector leaders." Later changes and additions to this group have resulted in the following alignment:

Doug and Joyce Arthur
British Commonwealth
Steve & Lisa Johnson
Eastern U.S.,
Caribbean, Africa
Randy and Kay McKean
New England,
Continental Europe
Pedro and Laura Garcia-Bengochea
Central and
South America
Frank and Erica Kim
The Pacific Rim
Scott and Lynn Green
China
Marty and Chris Fuqua
Midwest,
Western U.S.,
Canada,
Russia, C.I.S.
Cory and Megan Blackwell
Middle East
Al and Gloria Baird
Law and Media
Bob and Pat Gempel
HOPE worldwide

The magnitude of this movement is just now dawning on church historians. In only 18 years, God, working through the original men and women of the Boston church, has planted churches around the world who are planting churches who are planting even more churches. From 30 members in one small congregation to 120,000 meeting on Sunday mornings in more than 275 congregations in nearly every major city on every continent, the ministries are multiplying at an incredible rate just as Jesus commanded. Under the leadership of Kip and the world sector leaders, the movement has united behind the commitment to plant at least one church in every nation that has a city of at least 100,000 by the end of the year 2000, and to build "super churches" in the "super cities" of the world that their vast populations may be reached. In the fall of 1996 there were 31 dynamic churches throughout the world averaging more than 1,000 people in attendance each Sunday in these cities.

The challenge of church history from the first century until now for the modern disciple is: to always remain true to Christ, the Bible and his purpose, until people from "every tribe and language and people and nation" have been redeemed (Revelation 5:9). For those of us in God's modern movement, we "cannot help speaking about what we have seen and heard" (Acts 4:20) as we press on with our radical, "foolish" efforts to preach Christ where he is not known. Gamaliel's words should ever echo in our minds. If we were ever to slip into weak imitation of true Christianity, we would soon repeat history, walking the doomed path of tradition and eventual apostasy. May we never find ourselves fighting God, but fighting together for him. With his power we will see the world evangelized in our generation (Matthew 28:19-20). And to God be the glory!

[*Editors' note: The story goes on from here as you write history with your lives into the twenty-first century, the Lord willing.*]

International Churches of Christ in the United States by State

(April 1997)

Alabama
Birmingham
Alaska
Anchorage
Arizona
Flagstaff
Phoenix Valley
Tucson City
Arkansas
Little Rock
California
Bakersfield
Fresno
Los Angeles
Sacramento
San Diego
San Francisco
Colorado
Colorado Springs
Denver
Connecticut
Groton/New London
Hartford
Florida
Tampa Bay
Jacksonville
Miami
Orlando
Tallahassee

Georgia
Atlanta
Guam
Agana
Hawaii
Hilo
Maui
Oahu
Idaho
Boise
Illinois
Bloomington/Normal
Champaign
Chicago
Indiana
Indianapolis
Iowa
Des Moines
Kansas
Kansas City
Wichita
Kentucky
Louisville
Louisiana
New Orleans
Maine
Portland
Maryland
Baltimore
Massachusetts
Boston
Springfield
Worcester

Michigan
Detroit
Minnesota
Minneapolis/St. Paul
Missouri
Kansas City
St. Louis
Montana
Missoula
Nebraska
Lincoln
Omaha
Nevada
Las Vegas
New Hampshire
Nashua/Manchester
New Mexico
Albuquerque
New York
Albany
Buffalo
New York City
Syracuse
North Carolina
Charlotte
Raleigh/Durham/
Chapel Hill
North Dakota
Fargo
Ohio
Cincinnati
Columbus
Cleveland

Oklahoma
- Oklahoma City
- Tulsa

Oregon
- Portland

Pennsylvania
- Philadelphia
- Pittsburgh

Puerto Rico
- San Juan

Rhode Island
- Providence

South Carolina
- Charleston
- Columbia

South Dakota
- Sioux Falls

Tennessee
- Knoxville
- Memphis
- Nashville

Texas
- Austin
- Dallas/Ft Worth
- El Paso
- Houston
- San Antonio

Utah
- Salt Lake City

Vermont
- Burlington

Virgin Islands
- St. Thomas Island

Virginia
- Norfolk

Washington
- Seattle

Washington, D.C.
- Washington, D.C.

West Virginia
- Morgantown

Wisconsin
- Milwaukee

Wyoming
- Cheyenne

International Churches of Christ Non-U.S. Churches by Country
(April 1997)

Argentina
Buenos Aires
Australia
Adelaide
Brisbane
Gold Coast
Melbourne
Perth
Sydney
Austria
Vienna
Bahamas
Nassau
Bamako
Bamako
Barbados
Bridgetown
Belarus
Minsk
Belgium
Brussels
Bolivia
La Paz
Brazil
Belo Horizonte
Rio de Janeiro
Sao Paulo
Botswana
Gaborone
Bulgaria
Euro 3
Burkina Faso
Ougadougou
Cambodia
Phnom Penh
Cameroon
Douala
Canada
Calgary
Montreal
Ottawa
Toronto
Vancouver
Chile
Santiago
China
Red Dragon 1
Red Dragon 2
Red Dragon 3
Red Dragon 4
Colombia
Bogota
Congo
Brazzaville
Cook Islands
Rarontongo
Costa Rica
San Jose
Croatia
Euro 4
Curacao
Willemstad
Czech Republic
Prague
Denmark
Copenhagen
Dominican Republic
Santo Domingo
Ecuador
Quito
England
Birmingham
Bristol
Leeds
Liverpool
London
Manchester
Oxford
Estonia
Tallin
Ethiopia
Addis Ababa
Fiji Islands
Fiji
Lautoka
Suva
Finland
Helsinki

France
- Lyon
- Marseille
- Paris

Georgia
- Tblisi

Germany
- Munich
- Dusseldorf
- Berlin

Ghana
- Accra

Greece
- Euro 1

Guatemala
- Guatemala City

Guyana
- Georgetown

Haiti
- Port-Au-Prince

Honduras
- San Pedro Sula

Hong Kong
- Hong Kong

Hungary
- Budapest

India
- Ahmedabad
- Bangalore
- Bombay
- Calcutta
- Cochin
- Coimbatore
- Goa
- Hyderabad
- Kottayam
- Madras
- New Delhi
- Pune
- Ranchi
- Trivandrum

Indonesia
- Jakarta
- Manado
- Medan
- Pontianak
- Surabaya

Ireland
- Dublin

Italy
- Milan

Ivory Coast
- Abidjan
- Dolea
- Ougadogou

Jamaica
- Kingston

Japan
- Fukuoka
- Nagoya
- Osaka
- Tokyo

Kazakhstan
- Alma-Ata

Kenya
- Eldoret
- Nairobi

Kyrgyzstan
- Bishkek

Laos
- Vientiane

Latvia
- Riga

Lithuania
- Vilnius

Malaysia
- Kuala Lumpur
- Johor Bahru
- Penang

Mexico
- Guadalajara
- Monterey
- Mexicali
- Mexico City
- Puebla
- Tijuana

Moldova
- Kishinev

Mongolia
- Ulaanbaatar

Myanmar
- Myanmar

Namibia
- Windhoek

Nepal
- Kathmandu

Netherlands
Amsterdam
New Zealand
Auckland
Christchurch
Nigeria
Ilorin
Lagos
Warri
Norway
Oslo
Papua New Guinea
Port Moresby
Paraguay
Asuncion
Asuncion International 1
Philippines
Bacolod City
Cagayan De Oro
Daan Bantayan (N. Cebu)
Davao
General Santos
Laoag City
Legaspi City
Baguio
Batangas
Cebu
Manila
Olongapo City
Zamboanga
Poland
Warsaw
Portugal
Euro 2
Romania
Bucharest
Russia
Ashkhabad
Minsk
Moscow
Nizhny Novgorod
Novosibirsk
St. Petersburg
Vladivostok
Yekaterinburg
Scotland
Edinburgh
Singapore
Singapore
South Africa
Cape Town
Durban
Johannesburg
Maputo
Port Elizabeth
Umtata (Transkei)
South Korea
Pusan
Seoul
Taegu
Spain
Madrid
Sri Lanka
Colombo
Suriname
Gemeente Van Christus
Sweden
Stockholm
Switzerland
Zurich
Geneva
Taiwan
Hsin Chu
Taipei
Thailand
Bangkok
Trinidad and Tobago
Port of Spain
Turkmenistan
Ashkhabad
Ukraine
Kharkov
Kiev
Odessa
Uzebekistan
Tashkent
Vietnam
Ho Chi Minh City
Zaire
Kinshasa
Zambia
Luzaka
Zimbabwe
Harare

Recommended Reading List

For the most part, the following reading list was compiled by kingdom teachers at a meeting in Wells, Maine, in November 1995. Obviously, some works have to be recommended with qualifications.

REFERENCE BOOKS

Newer Disciples:

1. Concordance (Complete)
2. Topical Bible (Naves—new edition)
3. *Thompson's Chain-Reference Bible*
4. *Encyclopedia of the Bible* (British version: Lions)
5. *Handbook to the Bible* (American version: Eerdmans)
6. *True and Reasonable* by D. Jacoby (DPI)
7. *The Friendship Factor*, Alan Loy McGinnis
8. *A Tale of Three Kings,* Gene Edwards
9. *Mark of the Lion Series (three novels),* Francine Rivers (Tyndale House)
10. *The Disciplined Life*, Richard Shelley Taylor
11. *Trusting God,* Jerry Bridges (NavPress)
12. *Know Why You Believe*, Paul Little
13. *The Victory of Surrender*, Gordon Ferguson (DPI)
14. Optional: *Wordsearch* (Navpress)—Computer program
15. The Daily Power Series (multi-volume works by DPI)
16. *Friends and Lovers*, Sam and Geri Laing (DPI)
17. *Raising Awesome Kids*, Sam and Geri Laing (DPI)

Maturing Disciples/Leadership Level:

1. *Vine's Expository Dictionary of NT Terms* (new edition)
2. *New Bible Dictionary*—3rd edition, edited by J.D. Douglas (IVP)
3. *Early Christians Speak* by Everett Ferguson (Sweet)
4. *Prepared to Answer* by G. Ferguson (DPI)
5. *Eerdman's Handbook of a History of Christianity*, edited by Tim Powdey
6. *Understanding Non-Christian Religions* by McDowell and Stewart (Here's Life)
7. *He Walked Among Us* by Josh McDowell
8. *What if Jesus Had Never Been Born?* James Kennedy
9. *Will the Real Heretics Please Stand Up* by David Bercot (Scroll Publishing Co.)
10. *The Master Plan of Evangelism*, Robert Coleman
11. *Spirit Controlled Temperament*, Tim LaHaye
12. *Spiritual Leadership*, J. Oswald Sanders
13. *Power Through Prayer*, E. M. Bounds
14. *The Self-Study Guides (series),* Irving Jensen
15. *The Lion Never Sleeps*, Mike Taliaferro (DPI)
16. The Practical Exposition Series (Four volumes by DPI)

Early Ministry:

1. *New Testament Survey* by Merrill Tenney
2. *How We Got the Bible* by Neil Lightfoot

3. *The Documents of the New Testament: Are They Reliable*? by F.F. Bruce (Eerdmans)
4. *Mere Christianity* (C.S. Lewis)
5. *Basic Christianity* by John Stott (Eerdmans)
6. *Evidence That Demands a Verdict* by Josh McDowell
7. *The Anchor Bible Dictionary* (6 volumes)
8. *The MacMillan Bible Atlas*
9. *Basic Principles of Biblical Counseling* by Larry Crabb (Zondervan)
10. *Powerful Preaching Made Practical* (Booklet and tape set by G. Ferguson (DPI)
11. *A Theology of the NT* by George E. Ladd (Eerdmans)
12. *Tyndale Commentary* set
13. *The Jesus I Never Knew* by Philip Yancey (Zondervan)
14. *Baptism in the NT* by G.R. Beasley-Murray (Eerdmans)

Teacher Level:

1. *The Spreading Flame* by F.F. Bruce
2. *Christians Only* by James Deforest Murch
3. *The Universe Next Door* by James Sire (IVP)
4. *Theological Dictionary of the* NT, ed. by Colin Brown (Zondervan)
5. *Cynic, Sage or Son of God* by Gregory Boyd
6. *Interpretation of the NT* by Stephen Neill
7. *Introduction to the NT* by Drane
8. *Linguistic Key to the Greek NT* by Bruce Metzger
9. *Survey of the OT* by Bush and Hubbard
10. *Jesus and Christian Origins Outside the NT* by F.F. Bruce
11. *The OT Apocrypha* (Oxford University Press)
12. *Historical Criticism of the Bible*, Eta Linnemann (Baker)

Frequently Asked Questions About the International Churches of Christ

The following material is taken from the Official World Wide Web Page of the International Churches of Christ and is used here by permission. That page can be found at **www.icoc.org**.

What makes the International Churches of Christ unique?

There are several things that make us unique. First, we are committed to continually searching the Bible for truth about our lives and God's will for us as His church. Second, we believe and expect every member of the church to be fully committed to living according to that truth. These convictions, as straightforward and obvious as they may seem, do not characterize the convictions of most of the religious world around us.

To our knowledge, we are the only group that teaches the biblical principle of discipleship as a necessary part of the salvation process. We believe that an individual is not a candidate for baptism, and, therefore, salvation, unless he or she is ready to repent of sin and make the commitment to live each day of his or her life as a disciple of Jesus Christ.

Another unique quality of our churches is the diversity found in our fellowship. Sadly, it has been observed that Sunday morning is the most segregated time of the week for most Americans. Most churches only talk about diversity; we live it. We believe that any religious group that allows racial, social or economic segregation does not reflect the unity and love of God our Father and, therefore, cannot be the true church of Jesus Christ. God's true church is made up of all kinds of people, coming together as one common body to share one common love.

What is your mission?

Jesus said in Luke 19:10 that he came "to seek and save what was lost." Because of this purpose he commanded his disciples to "Go and make disciples of all nations, baptizing them in the name of the Father and of the Son and of the Holy Spirit, and teaching them to obey everything I have commanded you. And surely I am with you always, to the very end of the age" (Matthew 28:19-20). Therefore, as disciples of Jesus, our mission is to "make disciples of all nations."

What are you doing to fulfill your mission?

Fulfilling Jesus' mission involves several important things:

First, in order to make disciples of all nations, the church must be composed of disciples willing to go to every nation. The International Churches of Christ began our commitment to this in 1982 by sending mission teams from our church in Boston to Chicago and London. Amazingly, fifteen years later there are nearly 300 churches in more than 100 nations. Our short term goal is to plant a church in every nation with a city of at least 100,000 people by the year 2000.

Second, fulfilling Jesus' mission is possible only when we are committed to the preaching and teaching of God's Word, the Bible. As Jesus stated in Matthew 28:20, we must teach all nations to obey everything that he commanded. Powerful, practical and knowledgeable preaching and teaching which calls people to live obedient lifestyles are absolutely necessary to the making of true disciples.

Third, fulfilling Jesus' mission involves following his example in meeting the physical, emotional, and spiritual needs of those around us. During his ministry, Jesus healed large numbers of people with all types of diseases. When he saw crowds of people " he had compassion on them" (Matthew 9:36). Likewise, we as disciples of Jesus in the 20th century are striving to have the same compassion for the people of the world.

Why is the church growing so rapidly?

The International Churches of Christ have grown in Sunday attendance from less than 100 in 1979 to over 140,000 today. This growth is certainly remarkable, especially when you consider that in all of our churches the attendance significantly exceeds the membership of the church. Few churches in the religious world have an attendance that even approaches their membership, much less exceeds it.

The church described in the Bible grew for a couple of basic reasons. First, it preached the message of Jesus Christ, and secondly, the early disciples were deeply committed to see that this message was spread throughout the world. We believe that our churches are growing today for the same reasons. People are looking for something in life beyond materialism and pleasure. They want to find a meaningful purpose and lasting relationships. Christ's teachings provide those very things. A return to biblical principles in our day yields the same results as in the first century, deep relationships with God and one another and a genuine purpose in life.

Who attends the International Churches of Christ?

All kinds of people! People of all ages, all cultures, all economic levels, all religious backgrounds and every kind of past are made to feel welcome in our fellowship. For instance, our largest congregation, the Los Angeles Church of Christ, has a Sunday attendance of more than 11,000 of which 33% are married, 33% are single, 22% are college students, 6% are teens, and 5% are single parents. Visitors often comment on the racial diversity in both our membership and our leadership. In a day when younger people are abandoning traditional religion, people are also impressed with the large numbers of vibrant youth in our churches.

How do you help the poor and needy?

Just as Jesus had compassion on the poor and the sick, we teach and believe that all disciples should give of themselves to serve the poor where they live. In 1987, a fresh study of the Scriptures brought us to the conviction that this was an area of God's will that we had largely neglected. Since then our churches have worked hard to repent and correct this problem. Each church in our fellowship now reaches out into its own community with various projects to help those who are less fortunate.

In order to serve larger needs around the world, a coordinated outreach, called HOPE *Worldwide*, was begun. This organization has grown to include more than 100 projects over 30 nations around the world. Most of our churches support HOPE Worldwide by providing generous financial help and by supplying enthusiastic volunteers. Several projects (such as a modern housing project for lepers in India, and HOPE for Kids Immunization Program in the USA) have gained national and international acclaim. But whether the work is a large, high-profile project or a simple helping of one person by another, our goal is to imitate

Jesus in his concern for the poor and needy and to make a difference in every way that we can!

The religious world seems to be plagued with sexual and financial scandals. How are you different?

The Bible makes it clear that church leaders must be people of character whose lives are worthy of respect and imitation. Therefore, we have the highest expectations of integrity and purity for those serving as leaders in the International Churches of Christ. Leaders in our church do not have extravagant lifestyles. All full-time workers, including the leadership of the ICC, are paid according to a standardized salary model that is reviewed for reasonableness and fairness by an independent consulting firm specializing in non-profit organizations. Our congregational finances are managed by professional financial administrators and not by the ministry staff. This means that the ministers, while being involved in the financial planning for the church, have no authority to write checks or disburse funds. Each congregation's financial and legal affairs are under the supervision and scrutiny of a corporate board composed of qualified members of the local churches. In order to further assure the integrity of our church finances, our largest churches are audited annually by independent outside accounting firms.

The Bible teaches that there is no one who is beyond temptation and sin, and certainly leaders are no exception. All full-time leaders in our church are expected to have people of strength, character and integrity involved in their personal lives. These are people to whom they are consistently accountable and with whom they openly discuss their weaknesses, faults and temptations. While our leaders are committed disciples of Jesus, we realize they are human and like all of us, still sin. As with any member, biblical counsel and discipline are available to help leaders in their struggles. Through the years there have been isolated cases of leaders becoming involved in immorality, drunkenness or other grave sins. All were given the help needed to assist in overcoming their problems. In some cases, it was necessary to remove them from leadership. With these kinds of safeguards in place, it is our hope that we may maintain a standard of conduct that will cause our churches, as described in TIME magazine, to continue to be "unbesmirched by financial and sexual scandals" (TIME, May 18, 1992).

What is the role of women in your church?

It is our belief that women should be as prominent and valued in our churches as they were in Jesus' ministry. Jesus was the greatest liberator of women the world has ever seen. In a day and time in which women were commonly regarded as inferior or as mere possessions to be owned, used and discarded, he treated all the women in his life with respect and dignity. We believe that Christian women have the same mission as men — to change the world by making disciples of Christ. While Scripture instructs us not to put women in positions of authority over men (1 Timothy 2:12), they are to serve beside men in the work of the gospel (see Romans 16:1-16), as well as functioning as powerful leaders of other women (Titus 2:3-4). While some of their roles may be different from men, women are viewed by God as equals to their male counterparts (Galatians 3:28). Many of those visiting our congregations are struck by the vibrant, joyful, dynamic women in our membership and leadership. Adherence to these scriptures has produced a powerful women's ministry in our churches that has given our women a sense of confidence and a place of influence that has too long been denied them in the religious world at large. This has all been brought about by our return to the simple, but revolutionary teaching of Jesus - that women and men in his church are disciples—first, foremost and always!

How are the activities of the International Churches of Christ funded?

Activities of the International Churches of Christ are funded by generous giving of the individual members themselves. Each Christian's duty to give is clearly spelled out in such passages as 1 Corinthians 9:1-12, and every member is expected to contribute sacrificially to the work of the church.

In most of our congregations there are two types of contributions. The first is the weekly contribution at which time members are encouraged to tithe — that is, give 10% of their income. While some members cannot afford to contribute 10% (though it is hoped they will be able to do so when their financial condition improves), many give more; it is up to each member to decide how much they give. The second contribution is an annual missions contribution, which primarily supplies needs of congregations in the Third World although some funds are used for mission work in other first and second world countries and for local needs. This offering averages about one-third of each member's total annual weekly contribution. In the ICC there is no income from investments, real estate or "front organizations" typical of some religious groups. Therefore, members' offerings are the sole means of funding the work of both overseas missions and domestic churches. Since fewer than 2% of congregations own buildings, money collected does not go to pay for lavish, impractical facilities with their accompanying high mortgages and overhead. Rather the majority of funds go to increase numbers of ministry staff or to other projects that are directly involved in ministering to people's needs. The financial responsibilities of church membership are clearly taught and explained before someone becomes a member of the church, and questions by members about procedures and allocation of funds are welcomed.

What do you expect of your members?

We expect all of our members to love God with all their hearts, all their souls and all their minds and to love their neighbors as they love themselves. (Matthew 22:37). All church members must be disciples of Jesus who accept his teachings as a daily standard for life. We do not believe discipleship is optional for our members. Furthermore, every disciple must seek to develop a growing, personal relationship with God and minister to the needs of those all around him. Clearly, we believe God expects us to love and serve with a commitment far beyond what most of us have typically observed in the religious world (Romans 12:10, 1 John 3:16).

What time commitment is involved as a member of the church?

This is an important question since the average member of our fellowship is significantly more involved in the work of the church (Ephesians 4:16) than most men and women in the religious world at large. Generally speaking, there are about six hours of meetings per week. In addition, members spend time with their Christian friends in informal fellowship and friendship settings outside of the regular church meetings. Is this excessive? Absolutely not! Most denominations hold several different meetings per week: worship services, Sunday school classes, midweek meetings, prayer meetings and so forth — and the more committed members attend all of them. And when all members attend all the meetings this is highly lauded. In our congregations when the average member comes to all the meetings it certainly should not be regarded as unusual behavior. Why? Because the Bible tells us that the early Christians were willing to meet daily (Acts 2:46). Moreover, for anyone who considers the time commitment unreasonable, take note that the average American adult according to USA Today watches a staggering 28 hours a week of TV! Christianity is a religion of action, a lifestyle of a relationship to God and others.

What does the term "being discipled" mean?

Jesus taught his own disciples to go into the world and make other disciples. This involved older or more mature disciples teaching and training young converts to become more like Jesus. Being "discipled" simply means getting input, advice and teaching from people we know and respect so that each one of us can become more like Jesus. Being "discipled" does not mean that someone else makes our decisions for us nor does it mean blindly doing whatever we are told. Discipling is based on a relationship of trust, friendship and closeness, and breaks down if the people involved do not become great friends who respect and appreciate each other's faith, love and individuality. In our churches we work hard to make sure that all disciples have at least one person who helps them to have a Christ-like perspective, to make needed changes, and to get the encouragement needed to live the Christian life.

How does being a member of the International Churches of Christ help other areas of life such as career and family?

God calls disciples to do their best at whatever they do (Colossians 3:23). For example, the Bible teaches disciples to be excellent employees - to be honest, eager, productive and hard-working. Family life is another top priority. Husbands and wives are called to build the best marriages possible with God at the center, whether or not their spouses are disciples. Parents should rear their children in an atmosphere of love, teaching them to love God, to love life, and to set great examples in their efforts in the classroom and in other school and community activities. Disciples should love and honor their parents, even if their parents are not disciples and are not supportive of their pursuit of God and their involvement in the church. Sadly, many people today have been affected by dysfunctional marriages and families. One of the greatest joys of our fellowship is to see broken, hurting marriages mended and healed through the power of the love of Christ. We also strive to see children and parents reunited in love for each other through the forgiveness and hope that Jesus brings into their lives. We teach our couples to build close, loving marriage relationships and to raise their children in a secure, loving family. One of the most noticeable aspects of our fellowship is the happy marriages and joyful households that have been produced by our emphasis on biblical family life. Incredibly, in our seventeen year history, divorce is very rare among those who have been married in the International Churches of Christ.

Do you believe that your church is perfect?

Not at all. Only God is perfect. We are simply sinners who have been saved by the grace of God and who are striving to please God in all that we do. Unlike some groups that espouse the doctrine of "sinless perfection," we claim neither the church nor any individual in the church to be "perfect." However, that does not mean that apathy is acceptable! Jesus made that very clear in Revelation 3:15-16 when he rebuked lethargy and commended earnestness. In 1 John 1:7-10 we see that God expects us to walk in the light. Yet we will still sin, and in his grace he has made provision for that through the sacrifice of Jesus Christ on the cross. Moreover, we do not believe that our leaders are perfect. Even the great apostle Paul admitted as much in Philippians 3:12-13. Although we hold very high standards for our leaders, they still make mistakes. The thousands of leaders around the world are certainly going to make a number of mistakes, even while having the best of intentions. Grace is a daily reality for the disciple of Jesus. Each true follower of Jesus is willing to admit his or her sin, repent and rejoice in the love of God. Disciples grow as they change to be more like Jesus.

Are you teaching salvation by works?

No! We teach that salvation is by the grace of God and was purchased by Christ's death on the cross (Ephesians 2:8-10, 1 Corinthians 1:21-24). There is no deed or deeds we can do that are sufficient to earn us God's forgiveness or pay for the debt of our sin. Sin can be forgiven only through the blood of Christ (Romans 3:23-26). We do preach the biblical doctrine of repentance from sin and that true biblical faith results in obedience (Romans 1:5). The Bible teaches that without a changed and committed life, our faith is dead and does not lead to salvation (James 2:14-26).

You Made the Right Decision

(Especially for new Christians)

by Thomas A. Jones

> *But you are a chosen people, a royal priesthood, a holy nation, a people belonging to God, that you may declare the praises of him who called you out of darkness into his wonderful light. Once you were not a people, but now you are the people of God; once you had not received mercy, but now you have received mercy.*
> *1 Peter 2:9-10*

My new Christian friend, this is written especially for you to help you understand what you have done and what you have become. Some time ago, you did what few in this world ever do. You made a decision that few have the courage to make. You left one life behind and burst into a new life, whose architect and designer is God. You turned your back on the "wisdom of this world," on that which you had been taught for years, on that which had become such a part of you that you didn't know for a very long time that there was any other way to be, and you reached out and embraced the wisdom of God. You did what few have the integrity and the guts to do.

Not even those who skydive or climb mountains or race into battle do something as daring as you did. You left the familiar, the normal, the traditional and the expected and you cast your lot with a radical. You didn't do it to be a rebel, because he didn't do what he did to be a rebel. You did it because it is right. You did it because he is right.

You did it because you came to your senses. You did it because your eyes were opened. You did it because you saw that it is not in man to direct his own steps. You did it because you saw and understood that apart from God we can do nothing. You gave yourself to Jesus Christ. You stood before others and you said for all to hear, "Jesus is Lord." Those words of yours echoed all the way to the corners of glory *and* into the dungeons of demons, because you stood face to face with the truth about God, the truth about yourself and the truth about this world, and you had the heart and the humility to admit how much you needed him.

My friend, you did the right thing. You put your faith in the right person. You committed to the right cause. And you will not be sorry.

From Old to New

Oh, yes, you were a sinner. You were dead in your trespasses and sins. You followed the ways of the world and, yes, even the evil one who rules the dominion of darkness. You gratified the cravings of your sinful nature. You followed its desires and thoughts. And you will never be able to look down on anyone and say, "Well, at least I wasn't that bad." You were bad and you must never forget that. Your need for a savior was no less than the child-killer you read about in the newspaper or the sorry-looking figure you see in handcuffs on the evening news. Oh, your mother may have told you how nice you were and friends may have said you were wonderful, but none of them knew much about God's standards—his radical standards—his right and true standards. But you looked at and studied those standards with an open heart and saw yourself for the first time, and you cried out with the apostle, "Wretched man (or woman) that I am."

But then, by the grace of God, you made a right and courageous choice. You looked up into his eyes and said one of the most important words anyone can ever say to God. You said, "Help!" Like the Roman centurion, like the Canaanite woman, like the invalid at the pool, you said, "I need help." You said, "I need *your* help." And then God looked back at you and said, "I will help. I am in the helping business. I am in the saving business. I am in the redeeming business. I am in the forgiving business." And then God worked a miracle. He took a sinner who was lost in an empty way of life, traveling toward hell and without hope, and he made you new. And that is what you are today. You are new. You don't belong to the old any more. You belong to the new.

You confessed, "Jesus is Lord" and went down into the water. You were buried with Jesus in baptism and your *old* life was consigned to the grave (and by way, let it stay there). You came out of the water and are not the same. A new Spirit is filling you up. Heaven's view of you has changed and now your view of everything can change. Once you looked at things from a human point of view. Now you do so no longer. Everything Jesus did has now been applied to your life. Everything he achieved has been credited to your account. When God looks at you today, it is as though he is looking at Jesus. Incredibly, you stand before him without spot or blemish and free from accusation (and this remains true for as long as you live if you continue in your faith). The old has passed away. The old *you* is gone. The old record of sin is gone. The old sentence of death is gone. All things have become new. Take some time to just let that soak in. It is so amazing that you won't get it quickly. In fact, only in heaven will you surely understand it all.

Challenges Ahead

You have probably already learned that new does not mean perfect—at least not yet. (Perfect also must wait for heaven.) You are new, but there is still a lot of old around to deal with. You are new but you are not finished. There is still a great spiritual battle to be fought. You are on the right side. You have been given the right weapons. But there are some intense times ahead. One thing is for sure: Jesus never promises that following him will be a cushy ride. He promises life and joy and peace, but he also talks plainly about sacrifice, crosses, and persecution. He lets you know plenty of times that being new in an old world means there is a price to pay. But you counted the cost and with eyes wide open made your decision, and now by the grace of God you can keep paying the price as long as it takes.

Along the journey, you will have some great victories. You are fighting with a God who knows how to win. You will see amazing things. You've seen love, but you will see much more. You will see love that overcomes sin and love that overcomes hurt and love that never quits. You will have that kind of radical love for others and you will be loved with that kind of love. You are in a kingdom that is advancing around the world. You are in a church that is tearing down walls of division and bringing people together, and you will be a part of that. You will contribute to all this. God will take your talents, energize them with his Spirit and use you to make a difference in the lives of others.

God has a plan for your life and it will come true as you stay with him. He did not go to all the trouble of creating the world, choosing a nation, bringing a savior and giving us a Bible to let it all fizzle at the end of the twentieth century. What he starts he finishes, and what he started with you, he will finish. The bottom of the ninth and the fourth quarter always belong to God. He finishes, and he finishes strong.

But bear in mind that you will have some tough days. God allows them. Don't be surprised when they come. Don't despair if they come more often than you think they ought. Somehow they're all part of his plan to build your character. You'll have days when the demons of doubt will pound on your faith. You'll have days when the demons of fear chip away at your courage. You'll have days when the demons of selfishness will try to undermine your commitment. You'll have days when the demons of fatigue will tell you God expects too much. Your old life died with Christ in baptism, but the demons didn't take that same bath. You have a new mind and new heart but the demons haven't given up on reclaiming you for their cause.

Sometimes, they'll dress up in sheep's clothing and present their case in a dozen smooth and attractive ways. Sometimes they'll come dressed like football linebackers and try smashing you into hopelessness. Their minds are fertile with schemes to distract and discourage disciples. But mark this down: *No day will ever be so tough that you cannot make it through and no demon so strong that you cannot overcome him.* God just will not let it be any other way. You are his son or his daughter, and he will make sure that no matter how hot the fire, no matter how cold the wind, no matter how tough the disappointment, no matter how perplexing the question, he will always provide a way out—a way of escape—a way back to the one and only road that leads to heaven. Just make up your mind that you will never never never quit on God, and you can be sure that he will never quit on you.

Vital Principles

Being a disciple of Jesus is really a matter of taking very simple ideas and relentlessly applying them. And relentless means daily. Remember how often the word "daily" shows up in your Bible. Understand what that is saying about what we all need. Never think you can be an exception.

Your conviction that you needed help brought you to God in the first place. Now, let him hear from you every day how you need his help. *Make your prayer life a priority*. Do it now as a young disciple. Give it the place that it deserves—at the top of your "to do" list, at the center of your existence. But don't ever do it just to check it off. Don't do it to fulfill a duty. Do it because every day of your life as long as you live you will need help from God. Fight off the distractions, shake off the drowsiness, break out of the routine, do something unusual, but whatever it takes, claim your birthright. You are a child of the King. Walk with him every day. Lay every tough decision before him. Cast all your anxieties on him. Intercede with him for every person he is putting in your life to love. No matter how much you learn. No matter how much you do. No matter how many other great things others may say about you, learn to be a man of prayer or a woman of prayer and stay that way as long as you live.

And then, *treasure your Bible*. Expose your mind and your heart to it every day. In a world of shifting opinions and changing standards, it is your only safe guide to truth. When powerful feelings of sentimentality pull you toward compromise and an unbiblical broad-mindedness, the Bible will remind you that God means what he says. But beyond that you need the Bible's wisdom, its vision, its direction–and you need it fresh every day. If Jesus lived by every word that came from the mouth of God, how can we be any different?

And then look around you and *see the family you are in.* Be grateful for your physical family, but realize that this new spiritual family is even more of God. Here is where you will see godly examples. Here is where you will get godly advice. Here is where you will give and receive the love that Jesus said would get the attention of the world. And it needs to happen how often? There's that word again—daily. But remember, we haven't gotten to perfection yet. Your spiritual family is still on earth, not in heaven, which means you will have to forgive even as you will need to be forgiven. You will need to be forbearing, even as you will need others to be forbearing of you. But love this family. Treat it just the way God does.

And then, *never forget the importance of the mission.* Fulfilling the mission must be daily like the others. God has a strategy of getting his miracles into more offices, more neighborhoods, more cities, and more countries. You are at the center of his plan. He called you to fish for men and women, to go and help others become what you have become. You can think of a dozen reasons why you can't do it. But understand this: Your circumstances will change, your opportunities will change, your energy will change, your challenges will change. But your mission will not change. In every situation, you will still be Christ's ambassador and God will still be seeking to make his appeal through you. In many ways, being faithful here may be your greatest challenge, but aren't you grateful someone was faithful to you? Aren't you glad someone didn't make an excuse but found a way to get into your life and share with you that Jesus is Lord? Aren't you glad someone gave you a lot of time and stayed with you until you got it? Because that person did that for you, you can now do it for someone else. What that will mean to them and to you can hardly be described.

And so, my new Christian friend, you did the right thing. You have the right King. You are on the right road. You have the right friends. You are singing the right song and you are reading the right book. Never forget what you were, how you got here and who you belong to.

Weak or Uncommitted?

By Joe Woods

A very useful insight in evaluating our own lives and helping other Christians is learning to distinguish between a "weak" Christian and one who has simply become uncommitted to Jesus as Lord. The Scriptures provide clear answers concerning how to both identify and help Christians who are weak or uncommitted.

Characteristics of Being Weak

1. Limited in natural abilities or resources. 1 Corinthians 2:1-5; Judges 6:11-16.
2. Easily overtaken by problems and attitudes from non-Christian background. 1 Corinthians 8:4-7; Galatians 4:8-9.
3. Immature in understanding and limited in knowledge. Romans 14:1-15:6.
4. Trying hard, but making mistakes and blunders. Matthew 14:25-31; 16:21-23.
5. Making every effort to please God, but not relying on His power. Romans 7:14-25; Colossians 2:20-23.
6. Growing weary, losing heart, feeling discouraged. 2 Corinthians 11:24-30; Hebrews 12:1-12.

Ways to Help the Weak:

1. Accept and bear with them while they grow. Romans 14:1; 15:1.
2. Do not disdain or pass judgment on them. Romans 14:13; 1 Corinthians 8:1-2.
3. Do not cause to stumble by violating their conscience. Romans 14:13-21; 1 Corinthians 8:9-13.
4. Sympathize with them. 1 Corinthians 9:22.
5. Give them practical help. Acts 20:35; 1 Thessalonians 5:14.

Characteristics of the Uncommitted:

1. Lukewarm, halfhearted, giving partial effort. Revelation 2:4-5; 3:1-3; 3:15-16.
2. Not acknowledging one's own needs. Revelation 3:17-19.
3. Complacent, feeling a false sense of security. Isaiah 32: 9-11; Amos 6: 1.
4. Tuning out and ignoring God's message. Matthew 13:11-15; Hebrews 2:1-3.
5. Unteachable, close-minded. John 9:24-34; 2 Timothy 4:3-4.
6. Not using what one has been given. Matthew 25:24-27; Luke 12:47-48.
7. Self-centered, ignoring the spiritual and physical needs of others. Proverbs 24:11-12; Matthew 25:41-46; James 2:4-17; 1 John 3:16-18.
8. Laziness, unwillingness to work. 2 Thessalonians 3:6-13.
9. Being consistently unfruitful and unchanged. Proverbs 13:4; Matthew 21:43; Luke 13:6-9; John 15:5-6; 2 Peter 1:5-9.
10. Inconsistent participation in meetings of the body. Hebrews 10:24-25.
11. Making excuses when challenged. Luke 9:59-62; Luke 14:16-24.

Ways to Help the Uncommitted:

1. Call to repentance. Revelation 2:5; 3:3; 3:19.
2. Warn, then avoid. 1 Thessalonians 5:14; 2 Thessalonians 3:14-15.

As we attempt to help brothers and sisters who are weak or have become uncommitted, our goal is to help them decide for themselves whether they are weak or uncommitted. This can best be done by asking them specific questions which will cause them to recognize their spiritual condition. Examples of good questions are:

- Can you say you love God with all your heart, soul, mind, and strength?
- Are you seeking the kingdom of God first in every decision?
- Are you open to challenge and advice?
- Are you growing closer to God and becoming more like Jesus in your character? Do you find yourself often making excuses for not doing what you know is right?
- Would you characterize yourself as being hot, lukewarm or cold as a Christian?

These kinds of penetrating questions will expose the true spiritual condition of anyone if they are truthfully answered.

Those who are committed to God, even if weak, have an urgent desire to know God and be right with Him. (Psalm 27:4; Matthew 5:6; 2 Corinthians 5:9-10; Philippians 3:7-11) They make spiritual growth the top priority in their lives.

Characteristics of the Committed:

1. Teachable. Matthew 5:3; Acts 8:30-31.
2. Search God's word for themselves. Acts 17:11; Psalm 119:20, 24.
3. Pray consistently to have a right heart before God. Psalm 51:10-17.
4. Open in relationships. 1 Thessalonians 2:5-12.
5. Eager and consistent participation in the meetings of the body. Acts 2:42,46.
6. Taking initiative to put into practice God's will in their lives. Psalm 101:2-4; 1 Timothy 4:7.
7. Always being eager to repent of sin. 2 Corinthians 7:10-11.
8. Making "kingdom-first" decisions. Matthew 6:19-24, 33; Acts 20:24; 2 Corinthians 5:14-15.
9. Obvious progress toward maturity. Hebrews 5:11-6:1.
10. Conscious effort to acquire new skills and be more productive. Matthew 25:16-23; Ephesians 4:11-16.
11. Evidence in speech and life of total commitment. Matthew 12:33-37.

We need to continually be examining ourselves and helping others examine themselves concerning where we are spiritually. Lukewarmness and lack of commitment not only cause those who are lukewarm to be lost, but are discouraging to committed disciples. According to Revelation 3:15-16, God's order of preference is: (1) hot; (2) cold; (3) lukewarm. Many find it difficult to accept that being "cold" spiritually is better than being "lukewarm." But when we consider the tremendous harm to the cause of Christ which results from lukewarm Christians, we can begin to understand God's wisdom.

Six Places Baptism Shows Up

by Thomas Jones

Baptism is not the most important subject in the NT, but it is a vital one. This becomes clear when we notice where baptism shows up—right in the middle of some of the most crucial and vital Scriptures.

1. Matthew 28:18-20—baptism is right in the middle of the Great Commission. Jesus leaves his disciples and tells them what he most wants them to do.

2. Acts 2:36–38—baptism is the vital conclusion of Peter's Pentecost message. People convinced of Jesus and convicted of their sin are called to repentance and baptism.

3. Ephesians 4:1-4—baptism shows up right in the middle of "the seven ones." It is right there with one Lord, one faith, one God and Father.

4. Romans 6:1-4—baptism shows up in the midst of a key conversion passage. When Paul wants to make the point that those saved by grace will no longer continue in sin, he says in so many words, "Don't you remember what happened to you in your baptism? In baptism you died to your old life."

5. Galatians 3:26-27—baptism shows up in the midst of a key passage on Christian identity. When Paul wants to remind people of who they are, he reminds them of who they were baptized into.

6. 1 Peter 3:21—here baptism shows up in a vital passage comparing Christian salvation to deliverance in the OT flood. The passage clearly says, "baptism now saves you also."

Conclusion: If we judge baptism by the company it keeps, it is a vital element in God's plan to bring us to new life in Christ. If many religious people today were rewriting the Bible, they would never leave baptism in such vital passages. Its presence in these scriptures is unexplainable in view of their doctrinal positions. Certainly, baptism has meaning only as it is related to Christ, but precisely because it is related to Christ, it is an essential, vital and powerful experience for every disciple of Jesus.

A Dozen Passages to Help in Your Ministry

1. When you are discouraged by the lack of responses...

   2 Corinthians 4:1: Therefore, since through God's mercy we have this ministry, we do not lose heart.

   And...

   Galatians 6:9: Let us not become weary in doing good, for at the proper time we will reap a harvest if we do not give up.

2. When you are frustrated and impatient with someone...

   1 Timothy 1:16: But for that very reason I was shown mercy so that in me, the worst of sinners, Christ Jesus might display his unlimited patience as an example for those who would believe on him and receive eternal life.

3. When you are lacking motivation and desire...

   2 Corinthians 5:14-15: For Christ's love compels us, because we are convinced that one died for all, and therefore all died. And he died for all, that those who live should no longer live for themselves but for him who died for them and was raised again.

4. When you find it hard to have vision for someone...

   1 Corinthians 1:26-29: Brothers, think of what you were when you were called. Not many of you were wise by human standards; not many were influential; not many were of noble birth. But God chose the foolish things of the world to shame the wise; God chose the weak things of the world to shame the strong. He chose the lowly things of this world and the despised things—and the things that are not—to nullify the things that are, so that no one may boast before him.

5. When you are opposed or slandered...

   Matthew 5:11-13: "Blessed are you when people insult you, persecute you and falsely say all kinds of evil against you because of me. Rejoice and be glad, because great is your reward in heaven, for in the same way they persecuted the prophets who were before you.

   "You are the salt of the earth. But if the salt loses its saltiness, how can it be made salty again?"

6. When you meet resistance and pride...

   2 Timothy 2:24-25: And the Lord's servant must not quarrel; instead, he must be kind to everyone, able to teach, not resentful. Those who oppose him he must gently instruct, in the hope that God will grant them repentance leading them to a knowledge of the truth.

7. When you have done everything you know to do for someone...

   Colossians 4:12: Epaphras, who is one of you and a servant of Christ Jesus, sends greetings. He is always wrestling in prayer for you, that you may stand firm in all the will of God, mature and fully assured.

8. When you feel you need more love for someone...

   Ephesians 5:1-2: Be imitators of God, therefore, as dearly loved children and live a life of love, just as Christ loved us and gave himself up for us as a fragrant offering and sacrifice to God.

9. When a younger disciple has blown it...

   2 Corinthians 2:7-8: Now instead, you ought to forgive and comfort him, so that he will not be overwhelmed by excessive sorrow. I urge you, therefore, to reaffirm your love for him.

10. When you have blown it...

   1 John 1:7-9: But if we walk in the light, as he is in the light, we have fellowship with one another, and the blood of Jesus, his Son, purifies us from all sin.

   If we claim to be without sin, we deceive ourselves and the truth is not in us. If we confess our sins, he is faithful and just and will forgive us our sins and purify us from all unrighteousness.

11. When you feel fearful and timid...

   Acts 18:9: One night the Lord spoke to Paul in a vision: "Do not be afraid; keep on speaking, do not be silent."

   And...

   Hebrews 2:11: Both the one who makes men holy and those who are made holy are of the same family. So Jesus is not ashamed to call them brothers.

12. When you are tempted to be less than honest and forthright:

   2 Corinthians 4:2: Rather, we have renounced secret and shameful ways; we do not use deception, nor do we distort the word of God. On the contrary, by setting forth the truth plainly we commend ourselves to every man's conscience in the sight of God.

Ten Definitions to Help Us Sing with Understanding

Panoply

"But take to arm you for the fight, the *panoply* of God." (Soldiers of Christ Arise)

Panoply is from the Greek *panoplia [pan-* all, complete + *hopa* arms, armor] meaning a full suit of armor.

Bulwark

"A mighty fortress is our God, a bulwark never failing." (A Mighty Fortress)

*Bulwark [*MD *bolwerc, bole-* plank, + *werc* work] a solid wall-like structure raised for defense, breakwall, seawall.

Lord Sabaoth

"Christ Jesus it is He! Lord *Sabaoth* is His name." (A Mighty Fortress)

Lord *Sabaoth* is a term derived from Hebrew which means Lord Almighty. It is used once in the NT in James 5:4.

Repose

"On the Rock of ages founded, what can shake thy sure *repose*." (Glorious Things of Thee Are Spoken)

Repose is a term which means eternal rest.

t'assuage [to assuage]

"Who can faint while such a river ever flows their thirst *t'assuage.*" (Glorious Things of Thee Are Spoken)

Assuage means to put an end to by satisfying, relieve, quench.

Diadem

"Bring forth the royal *diadem* and crown him Lord of all." (All Hail the Power of Jesus' Name)

Diadem is a royal crown or headpiece.

Visage

"How does that *visage* languish, which once was bright as morn." (O Sacred Head)

Visage means appearance, face.

Cherubim and Seraphim

"Cherubim and *Seraphim* falling down before Thee." (Holy, Holy, Holy)

Cherubim is an order of celestial beings or angels. *Seraphim* is a specialized order of six-winged angels that attend to God on his throne (Isaiah 6:2-3,6-7).

Vintage

"He is trampling out the *vintage* where the grapes of wrath are stored." (Glory, Glory, Hallelujah)

Vintage is a season's yield of grapes or wine from a vineyard.

Aye

"My God and I will go for *aye* together." (My God and I)

Aye means forever, always, continually.

PART THREE

•Ideas•

Twelve Questions to Talk Over with a Discipleship Partner

For both:

1. Do we relate more as friends or more as "business associates?"
2. What can we do to take our friendship deeper?
3. Do we know each other's greatest challenges, struggles and fears?
4. Do we feel like *prayer* partners with one another?
5. What steps can we take to enrich our joint prayer life?
6. What do you think is the greatest strength in this relationship?
7. What is a weakness that needs attention?
8. What convictions do you have about discipling?

For the discipler:

9. Do you feel the person you are discipling is eager for your input?
10. Do you feel you are making it easy for him or her to be open with you?

For the one being discipled:

11. Are you making it easy for your partner to stay in touch with what is going on in your life?
12. Are you demonstrating eagerness and a great willingness to grow and change?

Couples' Discipling Times

A suggested way for couples to use their discipling times.

by Wyndham Shaw

1. **Commendations and compliments:** Share what you really have appreciated in each other – and make it a great time of encouragement!

2. **Areas of need and/or problems:** Share things that have bothered you about your mate. However, mention only one or two things per session. We are talking about having a discipling time, not a gripe session! Be sure to listen carefully without becoming defensive. No one knows you as well as your life partner. Therefore, be anxious to get their perspective and learn from them. Humility is required and humility will be rewarded (maybe in some very exciting ways!).

3. **Plan your calendar and schedules for the week** (or next week, if your discipling time is near the weekend). Talk about areas of shared responsibility such as child care, use of the car, and other areas needing coordination between the two of you.

4. **Talk about your feelings** – your goals, desires, dreams, frustrations, fears and anything else that really brings out your heart and inner convictions. For those who find sharing at this level difficult (are you listening, men?), some specific exercises may help to strengthen your "feeling-expressing muscles." One such exercise is to talk back through your lives together a year at a time. Anything you remember from the early years of your life is most likely remembered because it was associated with an emotional experience, either positive or negative. Sharing these memories together will bond you and increase your understanding and appreciation of your partner. Another exercise is to share with each other something you have never shared before. The more difficult it may be to share it, the more it will help the sharer and the marriage bond. Bottom line, learn to share your hearts together. Real intimacy is much more a matter of heart to heart than body to body.

5. **Household management:** Talk about needs around the house (the *Honey-do* list)!

6. **Children:** Talk about how you each are feeling about how the children are doing. Make sure that you are unified about *discipline* and other parenting concerns. Your unity as a couple in this area is more important than almost anything else. Stay spiritually focused and stay unified in dealing with your children.

7. **Plan for family devotionals:** Talk about the needs in the family and what scriptures would best meet those needs.

8. **Plan discipleship times** with each of the children during the week.

9. **Finances:** Make sure that adequate communication on all financial issues takes place, and that each of you feels unified about the financial decisions that are reached.

10. **Prayer:** Don't neglect the most important thing!

Forty Scriptures to Build Character in Children

Deuteronomy 6:5
Love the LORD your God with all your heart and with all your soul and with all your strength.

Luke 6:45b
"For out of the overflow of his heart his mouth speaks."

Luke 12:48b
"From everyone who has been given much, much will be demanded; and from the one who has been entrusted with much, much more will be asked."

Luke 14:11
"For everyone who exalts himself will be humbled, and he who humbles himself will be exalted."

John 14:15
"If you love me, you will obey what I command."

Romans 8:28
And we know that in all things God works for the good of those who love him....

Romans 12:17a
Do not repay anyone evil for evil.

1 Corinthians 10:13
No temptation has seized you except what is common to man. And God is faithful; he will not let you be tempted beyond what you can bear. But when you are tempted, he will also provide a way out so that you can stand up under it.

1 Corinthians 10:24
Nobody should seek his own good, but the good of others.

1 Corinthians 13:4-8a
Love is patient, love is kind. It does not envy, it does not boast, it is not proud. It is not rude, it is not self-seeking, it is not easily angered, it keeps no record of wrongs. Love does not delight in evil but rejoices with the truth. It always protects, always trusts, always hopes, always perseveres.
Love never fails.

2 Corinthians 10:5
...we take captive every thought to make it obedient to Christ.

Galatians 5:22-23a
But the fruit of the Spirit is love, joy, peace, patience, kindness, goodness, faithfulness, gentleness and self-control.

Galatians 6:9
Let us not become weary in doing good, for at the proper time we will reap a harvest if we do not give up.

Ephesians 4:32
Be kind and compassionate to one another, forgiving each other, just as in Christ God forgave you.

Philippians 2:3
Do nothing out of selfish ambition or vain conceit, but in humility consider others better than yourselves.

Philippians 2:14
Do everything without complaining or arguing…

Philippians 4:4a
Rejoice in the Lord always.

Philippians 4:13
I can do everything through him who gives me strength.

Colossians 3:20
Children, obey your parents in everything, for this pleases the Lord.

1 Thessalonians 5:16-18
Be joyful always; pray continually; give thanks in all circumstances, for this is God's will for you in Christ Jesus.

1 Timothy 4:12
Don't let anyone look down on you because you are young, but set an example for the believers in speech, in life, in love, in faith and in purity.

Hebrews 3:13
But encourage one another daily…

Hebrews 12:11
No discipline seems pleasant at the time, but painful. Later on, however, it produces a harvest of righteousness and peace for those who have been trained by it.

James 1:19
…Everyone should be quick to listen, slow to speak and slow to become angry…

James 1:22
Do not merely listen to the word and so deceive yourselves. Do what it says.

1 Peter 5:5
"God opposes the proud
but gives grace to the humble."

1 John 4:11
Dear friends, since God so loved us, we ought to love one another.

Joshua 1:7
"Be strong and very courageous."

1 Samuel 16:7b
"The LORD does not look at the things man looks at. Man looks at the outward appearance, but the Lord looks at the heart."

Psalm 119:9
How can a young man keep his way pure?
By living according to your word.

Psalm 139:23-24
Search me, O God, and know my heart;
test me and know my anxious thoughts.
See if there is any offensive way in me,
and lead me in the way everlasting.

Proverbs 3:7
Do not be wise in your own eyes....

Proverbs 6:16-19
There are six things the LORD hates,
seven that are detestable to him:
haughty eyes,
a lying tongue,
hands that shed innocent blood,
a heart that devises wicked schemes,

feet that are quick to rush
into evil,
a false witness who pours
out lies
and a man who stirs up
dissension among brothers.

Proverbs 11:25
...he who refreshes others will himself
be refreshed.

Proverbs 12:15
The way of a fool seems right to him,
but a wise man listens to advice.

Proverbs 13:24
He who spares the rod hates his son,
but he who loves him is careful to
discipline him.

Proverbs 17:22
A cheerful heart is good medicine,
but a crushed spirit dries up the
bones.

Proverbs 18:17
The first to present his case seems right,
till another comes forward and
questions him.

Proverbs 21:3
To do what is right and just
is more acceptable to the LORD than
sacrifice.

Ecclesiastes 7:14
When times are good, be happy;
but when times are bad, consider:
God has made the one
as well as the other.

Twenty-five Ways to Encourage Children

by Larry and Lea Wood

The encouragement of children is a key to the solving of discipline problems.

How to Encourage:

1. Emphasize the *deed*, not the doer.
2. Emphasize the *doing*, and the joy of doing.
3. Emphasize the *good part* of what they did.
4. Avoid saying "don't." Stress the *positive*.

Phrases That Encourage:

1. You are so good at... (You did good!)
2. Would you help plan this?
3. What would you think about ...
4. Some beginnings are difficult.
5. You are fun to be with. (I had a good time with you.)
6. Everyone makes mistakes.
7. I missed you...
8. I think ____ , but what do you think?
9. *Please,...*
10. That's a hard job.
11. I'm so glad that you had a good time in class today!
12. Let's see why it didn't work.
13. Don't ever let the things you can't do keep you from doing the things you can.
14. You did a great job on...(That's a great job!)
15. *Thank you* for...all your help to day, *Thank you* for saying that, do ing that, etc.
16. You're a hard worker! (You're a good helper!)
17. *I'm sorry* for...
18. That's great news!
19. You're special.
20. *I love you—I will always love you!*
21. I believe in you.

Six Great Family Devotionals

(Originally published in *His Children, 1990*)

1
Jesus Teaches Us to Be Honest

Clegg Dyson

Read Luke 19:1-10.

How many times have you said to a young child, "I told you to tell me the truth," and all you got back was a blank stare? As adults, we sometimes expect smaller children to understand the concepts of "truth" and "lying" well before they really can. But as children grow older, the concepts of being truthful or dishonest become very clear.

Dishonesty has become the world's "best policy!" We see it on TV, hear it on the radio, watch it on the movies. We are often taught that being dishonest and deceptive can spare hurting the feelings of others. How often have you heard a song which hints of telling little white lies? We are dishonest in hopes of getting away with something, but as the saying goes "what goes around, comes around." Lies will find us out. We will always be exposed even though it could take a long time before it happens.

Dishonesty is a learned sin. Young children are very honest and will tell the truth and will reap good and bad consequences. Once a child learns punishment accompanies acts of disobedience he has confessed, he will then try to conceal or lie about his actions in hopes of not being punished. But alas, Mom and Dad are smart, they used to do the same things as the children. We need to teach "honesty" from the very beginning. Honesty has great reward which far outweighs dishonesty. Honesty can determine our eternal destiny. Zaccheus' honesty brought him to Jesus. Honesty is the best "eternal policy."

Questions

1. Do you know why the people didn't like tax collectors?
2. Did the people like Zaccheus?
3. What did Zaccheus have to do in order to see Jesus?
4. What did Jesus say to him?
5. Was Zaccheus glad to be with Jesus?
6. What did Zaccheus decide to do after being with Jesus?
7. How did Zaccheus show his repentance?
8. What did Jesus say about Zaccheus and his decision?

Activity Ideas

During family devotional, talk about examples of honesty versus dishonesty. Discuss situations which best relate to the entire family. For example: chores done around the house. Did the children do what they were told? Were they honest about it? Discuss consequences of not telling the truth. Discuss the character of Jesus and that he always told the truth and that he expects us to do the same.

Admonition

Dishonesty is learned. Television can be a strong promoter of dishonesty in relationships, in being successful and in gaining material possessions. Please consider what your family is watching on television. Does it promote truth, or does it promote dishonesty? Parents should be very concerned and cautious about what the family views.

2
Say No to Evil

Becky Brand

Read Proverbs 25:26.

Before beginning this devotional, get a large clear glass containing clean water. Get one container of dirt or potting soil and a spoon. Put all of these on the floor in front of the children. Ask them to listen carefully as you read Proverbs 25:26. Have the children think of all the ways that we can use clean water everyday. They should name such uses as cooking, washing clothes, drinking, bathing and washing dishes.

Ask the children what it means to have polluted water. As you talk about the definition, stir in a spoonful of dirt into the clean water. Now, ask the children who would like to use this water to drink, to wash their dishes or to make lemonade. Surely no one would want to use this water! Polluted water is not good. It cannot be used for good purposes.

Proverbs 25:26 tells us that when we give in to evil we become "polluted. "Our hearts become polluted by evil things. God wants us to be righteous. Explain the definition of "righteous." To be righteous means that we do what is right. We want to be right with God and obey him daily.

Being righteous can be illustrated by the clean water. Help the children to understand that when our hearts are clean, we can be used in great ways by God, just as the clean water can be used by us in great ways. Evil can be illustrated by the polluted water. We cannot use the polluted water for good purposes. If we give in to evil daily, God cannot use us for all the great purposes he has for our lives.

Use the glass of water to continue illustrating the point of evil polluting our hearts. Let the children name ways they can get "dirt" into their "glasses" by giving in to evil. Each time they name something, stir in a spoonful of dirt into the glass. Some examples of giving in to evil or wrong influences around us would be:

1. We let our classmates persuade us to cheat on a test or our homework.
2. We lie to our parents or teachers because other kids are doing it.
3. We join the crowd in name calling or ex cluding classmates or other children from our group.
4. We accept someone's dare to steal toys, candy or gum.
5. We take God's name in vain because ev eryone else around us is doing it.
6. We are afraid the kids will laugh at us if we do not try to smoke; so we give in and try it.

The examples can be changed according to the ages and needs of your children. It's great to use examples of things you are working on with the children at the present time.

After the offenses have been named, go back through them one by one and have the children tell what they should do when they are tempted with each one. Their answers should be, "I will say, 'No.'"

Hold the glass of dirty water up so that the children can see it. This glass has a lot of dirt in it. But, it only takes a little dirt to spoil the whole jar. Remind the children that when they give in to evil and do the wrong thing, their hearts become like this dirty water. God wants us to be righteous. Tell the children, "Don't let any dirt get in your glass! Remember this glass the next time you are tempted to give in and do something wrong."

3
God Wants Us to Be Friendly

Betty Dyson

Read Romans 16:16; 1 Corinthians 16:19-20; 2 Corinthians 13:12-13.

Every parent has probably been very embarrassed and disappointed, at one time or another, by their child's lack of warmth and friendliness. God wants us to be friendly and warm to those around us. As parents, we need to set an example for our children to follow by being warm and friendly in our interactions with other people. We also must teach our children how to be friendly.

Read the scriptures listed above. What stands out in all of these verses? Christians send warm greetings. Explain to the children that to greet someone warmly means we are affectionate and enthusiastic when we see them. How do those around us feel when we approach them?

Activity

In order to help the children understand the importance of being warm and friendly, many different situations can be acted out.

Tell the children to enter the room and say, "Hello!" Your response is to totally ignore them and even make a face and turn your head. Have them continue to say "Hello," trying very hard to get your attention. Continue to ignore them, making it very obvious. Stop and discuss the situation. Ask the following questions:

1. How does it feel when you say "Hello" to someone and they ignore you?
2. How do you feel when someone turns his head away from you when you are trying to greet them?
3. How do you feel about yourself when someone ignores you and is not friendly at all to you?

Help the children to act out the situation again. You can sit on the couch, again, pretending to be at home. Have the children enter the room and say, "Hello!" This time your response is to jump up, smiling, run to them and hug them, saying, "Hello! I'm so glad to see you!" Stop and discuss the situation. Ask the following questions:

1. How does it feel when someone hugs you and tells you that they are glad to see you?
2. How do you feel about yourself when someone is very happy to see you, and they come to you and hug you and say "Hello."

Have the children act out other situations where they pretend to be the one at home, and you are the visitor. After acting out each situation, discuss their feelings.

Talk to the children about different friends of the family who come to your home often. Ask them questions like, "What should you do when Melanie comes in the door?"

Again, let them act out what they should do to greet the friend.

Parents, help your children to be friendly by reminding them how they felt when they were ignored in this devotional. Before a guest arrives at your home, remind the children how to greet them when the door is opened.

4

The Pharisee and Tax Collector Not Better Than Others

Greg Metten

Read Luke 18:9-14.

Activity Ideas

Older Children

Have these children write a dialogue between two people today which would express the same point contained in the parable. For example, are friends at school ever made fun of or teased because they look different, are a different race, have a different accent? Does this mean you are better than they? Do you look down on people who are not as cute, not as smart, not as well-dressed? Does God love them as much as He loves you? Have children make up a skit showing right and wrong ways to treat people who are different.

Younger Children

These children enjoy looking through magazines to discover ideas. Have them pick out pictures of people doing things that would make God happy. Glue all the pictures on a large piece of paper and put a title on it that the children select. When the picture is done, talk about each selection and show how it relates to being sincere in our love for God.

Practical Questions to Ask

Older Children

1. Why do we say things about others which would cause us to think we are better than they are?
2. The Pharisee was someone who did what God wanted him to do so he wouldn't get in trouble, rather than doing what was right because of his love for God and desire to please Him. What kinds of things do we do just because we don't want to get in trouble? What would be some examples of things we do out of love for someone else? Talk about the difference we feel inside in each of these cases.
3. What does it mean to be humble? If you're humble, does that mean you're weak? How can you be humble and strong at the same time?
4. Why is it so important to God that we don't think we're more important than we are?
5. Who was Jesus telling this parable to?

Younger Children

1. Why does it make God happy when we say we're sorry for something we've done?
2. When we go to church, it makes God very happy. What are some other things we can do to show God how special He is to us?
3. If (name one of child's friends) wants to play with our toys, how should we feel about that? What can we say to let him know we like to share with him?

Admonition

Look for ways each day to do things that are pleasing to God because you love him.

5
Respecting Authority

John Bringardner

Read the following scripture.
"For I, too, am a man under authority..."
Luke 7:8

Consider

Just mention the word "authority" and watch those around you dive for cover. Sadly, we live in a world where authority has been abused, confused and misused. Students thumb their noses at teachers, throw rocks at police and laugh at God. Authority has been shipwrecked on the rocks of disrespect because those in authority have failed to live up to the biblical standards of leadership. Thankfully, God has given us awesome examples of leadership both in his word and in his church. It is high time we reconsider what it means to respect authority.

Teach

Read Luke 7:1-10 aloud. Here, we find a man who understood what it meant to respect the authority of Jesus. Ask the children what it means to "respect" those who have authority over us. Respect means to pay attention to someone; respect means to obey. Help them to see that respect for authority involves "great faith" and is pleasing to Jesus! Ask the following questions:

1. Why did this man respect Jesus?
2. How did he show his respect for Jesus?
3. Why was Jesus amazed at this man?
4. Whom do we need to respect?
5. How can we show respect for authority?

Activity

Ask the children to perform a play with one child taking the role of someone in authority, i.e. policeman, teacher, etc. (This can be done as a "finger" play for families with only one child or little children.) Have the other family members act out showing disrespect for authority and then talk about how we should discipline such disrespect. Next, act out how we show respect for their authority, i.e. stopping for the policeman when he blows the whistle; sitting down when the teacher tells us, etc. Talk about why it is important to respect those who have authority. Share what authorities parents themselves must respect because God wants us all to show respect. Read Romans 13:1-7.

Have the parents and older children share about someone in the church they respect and why they respect them. Read Hebrews 13:7 and 17. Be sure to discuss how we respect those who are leaders in the church: our Bible Talk and House Church leaders; our elders, evangelists and women's ministry leaders. Share how we show respect for authority in the church. Take time to write a "family" note of thanks to someone in leadership. Pray and thank God for the leaders of the church.

6
Teaching Children to Pray

Kent Brand

Read John 11:41-44

How do you teach your children to pray? How do you instill a deep trust and confidence that God hears and answers our prayers? A powerful way is to show them that God will help them be victorious over any problem. I remember Joel's first day of kindergarten. Before he went to school he confided that he was "afraid." I immediately stopped what I was doing and said, "Let's talk to God about it." Joel had a successful day. Train your child where their security comes from by having "on the spot" prayers that relate to their fears and problems during the day.

Another anxious moment for our then fifth grader was the anticipation of his first oral book report. He really worked himself up into tears—afraid of the other children and what they might say. We prayed about the situation. Then after the report we were able to help him see it as a faith building time. Things went well and God blessed him.

'I have a problem'

Teach your child that God has the solution to every problem. Begin by singing, "Jesus Will Fix It" and "There's Not a Friend." Then ask the children, "Did you know that Jesus had problems?" Yes, Jesus was perfect but Satan tempted him like he does us. Did you know that Jesus had a friend named Lazarus who died? Even though Jesus was busy, he went to see the family. When he arrived he cried because he loved Lazarus so much. Jesus cared about his friend. He had a problem of a friend dying. Jesus cares about us.

Ask the children: What are your problems at school? In the family? In the neighborhood? Are you asking God to help you overcome your problems? In addition, name a specific problem each child has had within the last week: "Judy, you have had the problem of "feeling left out" this week. Tell me how does it feel? I want you to start praying everyday that you will make friends. Craig, you have had the problem this week of being afraid to give your book report. Does God care about how you feel? I want you to pray every day that God will help you to not be afraid."

'Let's pray'

Share with the children that when Jesus had a problem, the first thing he always did was to pray. Jesus prayed to God when Lazarus died. God answered his prayer and raised Lazarus from the dead. "Craig and Judy, what does God want us to do with our problems? Pray about them! Let's stop and pray now about your problems."

Give direction to each child in regard to praying for their specific problems. Share your specific problems you are praying for. Let each member of the family pray. "Craig and Judy, did God answer the prayer of Jesus, Yes, Lazarus came back from the dead."

Act out the story of Jesus raising Lazarus from the dead, then ask each person to share how God has answered prayer in their lives! Close the devotional sharing all the prayers that God will be answering: people becoming disciples, changes in families, and great victories for God.

Fifty Songs for Family Devotionals

1. AMEN

A—men, A—men
A—men, A—men, A—men.

See the little baby, lying in the manger,
Early in the morning.

See Him in the temple, talking to the elders,
How they marveled at His wisdom.

See Him at the seaside, preaching and healing, To the blind and feeble.

See Him in the garden, praying to the Father,
In deepest sorrow.

See Him there with Pilate, Pilate gave a choice.
But they wanted Barabbas.

See Him bear His cross now, up to Calvary.
Where they crucified my Lord.

See the empty tomb now, Christ has arisen.
And He lives with us today.

2. BUILDING UP THE KINGDOM

Building up the kingdom, building up the kingdom, building up the kingdom of the Lord
Brother, can you help me? Sister, can you help me?
Building up the kingdom of the Lord
It's so high, you can't get over it
So low, you can't get under it
So wide, you can't get around it
Gotta go through that door!
(repeat and speed up several times)

3. DEEP AND WIDE

Deep and wide, deep and wide,
There is a fountain flowing deep and wide.
Deep and wide, deep and wide,
There is a fountain flowing deep and wide.

4. DEEP DOWN IN MY HEART

I love the Lord Messiah...
deep down in my heart!
(repeat both lines)

CHORUS:
I said deep deep, down down
deep down in my heart! (repeat both lines)

2. I love to sing to Jesus...
3. I love to share my faith...
4. I want to be a disciple...
5. I want to pray to God...

5. DO LORD

I've got a home in glory land that out shines the sun.
I've got a home in glory land that outshines the sun.
I've got a home in glory land that outshines the sun.
Look away beyond the blue.

CHORUS;
Do, Lord, oh, do, Lord,
Oh, do remember me.
Do, Lord, oh, do, Lord, Oh,
do remember me.
Do, Lord, oh, do, Lord, Oh,
do remember me.
Look away beyond the blue.
I took Jesus as my savior;
You take Him too.
I took Jesus as my savior;
You take Him too.
I took Jesus as my savior;
You take Him too.
Look away beyond the blue.

I'm going to see my Jesus there
And you'll see Him too.

6. DON'T YOU WANNA GO TO THAT LAND?

Don't you wanna go to that land?
(repeat twice)
Where I'm bound, where I'm bound?
Don't you wanna go to that land?
(repeat twice)
Where I'm bound, where I'm bound?

2. Nothing but *love* in that land...
3. Nothing but *joy* in that land...
4. Nothing but *peace* in that land...
5. I've got a *Savior* in that land...

7. GIVE ME OIL IN MY LAMP

Give me oil in my lamp,
Keep me burning, burning, burning
Give me oil in my lamp I pray, (I pray)
Give me oil in my lamp,
keep me burning, burning, burning
Keep me burning till the break of day.

CHORUS
Sing Hosanna, Sing Hosanna,
Sing Hosanna to the King of Kings
Sing Hosanna, Sing Hosanna,
Sing Hosanna to the King

2. Give me love in my heart,
keep me loving, loving, loving
3. Give me joy in my heart,
keep me singing, singing, singing

8. GOD IS SO GOOD

God is so good. God is so good.
God is so good. He's so good to me.

God loves me so. God loves me so.
God loves me so. He's so good to me.

God answers prayers. God answers prayers.
God answers prayers. He's so good to me.

9. HARD FIGHTIN' SOLDIER

Lord, I'm a hard fightin' soldier on the battle-field.
(repeat twice)

CHORUS:
And I'll be bringing souls to Jesus,
By the service that I yield.

2. I've got a helmet on my head and in my hand a sword and shield.
3. You've got to walk right and talk right and sing right and pray right on the battlefield.
4. When I die, let me die in the service of my Lord.

10. HE'S GOT THE WHOLE WORLD

He's got the whole world in his hand (4x).

2. He's got you and me brother ...
3. He's got you and me sister ...
4. He's got _________ & ________....

11. I COULDN'T KEEP IT TO MYSELF

I said I wasn't gonna talk about it
But I couldn't keep it to myself,
Couldn't keep it to myself,
Couldn't keep it to myself,
Said I wasn't gonna talk about it,
But I couldn't keep it to myself,
What the Lord has done for me, for me.

CHORUS:
You oughta been there, (you oughta been there)
When He saved my soul, (saved my soul)
You oughta been there, (you oughta been there)
When He wrote my name on the roll;
I've started walkin', I've started talkin',
I've started singin', I've started shoutin'
What the Lord has done for me.

12. I HAVE DECIDED TO FOLLOW JESUS

I have decided to follow Jesus
I have decided to follow Jesus
I have decided to follow Jesus
No turning back, no turning back.

2. Though none go with me, still I will follow
3. The world behind me the cross before me
4. Will you decide now

13. I TRIED AND I TRIED

I tried and I tried, (Hallelujah),
I tried and I tried,
I tried and I tried, (Hallelujah),
until I found the Lord.

CHORUS:
My soul...(just couldn't be contented)
My soul...(just couldn't be contented)
My soul...(just couldn't be content)
Until I found the Lord.

2. I searched and I searched...
3. I prayed and I prayed...
4. I found, yes I found...I finally found the Lord.

14. IF I DON'T GET TO HEAVEN

If I don't (echo) get to heaven (echo)
If I don't (echo) get to heaven (echo)
If I don't get to heaven, dear Lord
It will be nobody, nobody, no-no-no-nobody's
Nobody's fault but mine.

2. If I don't read my Bible
3. If I don't share my faith
4. If I don't pray everyday
5. If I don't make disciples
6. If I don't get discipled

15. IF YOU'RE HAPPY AND YOU KNOW IT

If you're happy and you know it, clap your hands! (repeat)
If you're happy and you know it
then your life will surely show it
If you're happy and you know it, clap your hands!

2. Stomp your feet
3. Shout "Amen!"
4. Do all three!

16. I'M GONNA VIEW THAT HOLY CITY

I'm gonna view that holy city,
I'm gonna view that holy city
one of these days.
I'm gonna view that holy city,
I'm gonna view that holy city
one of these days.

2. I'm gonna meet my loving Jesus ...
3. I'm gonna sit at the welcome table ...
4. I'm gonna feast on milk and honey...
5. I'm gonna sing and never get tired ...

17. I'M HAPPY TODAY

I'm happy today, oh yes I'm happy today
in Jesus Christ, I'm happy today
because he's taken all my sins away
so that's why I'm happy today

2. I'm singing today
3. I'm praying today
4. I'm sharing today

18. I'M IN THE LORD'S ARMY

I may never march in the infantry,
Ride in the calvary, shoot the artillery.
I may never zoom over the enemy, but
I'm in the Lord's army.

I'm in the Lord's army. YES SIR!!
I'm in the Lord's army. YES SIR!!
I may never march in the infantry,
Ride in the calvary, shoot the artillery.
I may never zoom over the enemy, but
I'm in the Lord's army. YES SIR!!

19. IN AND OUT

I'm in right (point in)
Out right (point out)
Up right (point up)
Down right (point down)

HAPPY ALL THE TIME

Since Jesus Christ came in (point in)
And took away my sin (stretch out)
I'm in right (sing very fast using out right same motion)
Out right
Up right
Down right

HAPPY ALL THE TIME

20. IT ISN'T ANY TROUBLE

Oh, it isn't any trouble just to s-m-i-l-e
(repeat)
If ever you're in trouble
it will vanish like a bubble (pop!)
if you only take the trouble just to s-m-i-l-e!
1. P-R-A-Y
2. S-I-N-G
3. S-H-A-R-E
4. L-O-V-E

21. I'VE BEEN REDEEMED

I've been redeemed (echo)
By the blood of the lamb (echo)
I've been redeemed (echo)
By the blood of the Lamb
I've been redeemed by the blood of the Lamb,
Filled with the Holy Ghost I am.
All my sins are washed away,
I've been redeemed.
Well, I went down (echo)
To the river to pray (echo)
Well, I went down (echo)
To the river to pray.
Well I went down to the river to pray,
Felt so good that I stayed all day.
All my sins are washed away
I've been redeemed.

And that's not all (echo)
There's more besides (echo)
And that's not all (echo)
There's more besides.
And that's not all there's more besides,
I've been to the river and I've been baptized.
All my sins are washed away,
I've been redeemed.

22. I'VE GOT THE JOY, JOY, JOY

I've got the joy, joy, joy, joy
down in my heart (where?)
down in my heart (where?)
down in my heart
I've got the joy, joy, joy, joy
down in my heart
down in my heart to stay

CHORUS:
And I'm so happy, so very happy
I've got the Love of Jesus in my heart.
(Repeat Both Lines)

2. I've got the peace that passes understanding...
3. I've got the love of Jesus...
4. I've got the wonderful love of my blessed redeemer...

23. JESUS

Je—sus, Je—sus,
Jesus in the morning..
Jesus at the noontime,
Je—sus, Je—sus,
Jesus when the sun goes down.

Love Him, love Him,
Love Him in the morning,
Love Him at the noontime.
Love Him, love Him,
Love Him when the sun goes down.

Praise Him
Serve Him

24. JESUS CALLED THEM

Jesus called them one by one:
Peter, Andrew, James and John.
Next came Philip, Thomas too,
Matthew and Bartholomew.

CHORUS:
Yes, Jesus called them.
Yes, Jesus called them.
Yes, Jesus called them.
And they all followed Him.

James the one they call the less.
Simon, also Thaddeus,
Twelve apostles Judas made.
Jesus was by him betrayed.

CHORUS

25. JESUS LOVES ME

Jesus loves me, this I know,
For the Bible tells me so.
Little ones to Him belong,
They are weak but he is strong.

CHORUS:
Yes, Jesus loves me, (repeat twice)
The Bible tells me so.

Jesus loves me when I'm good.
When I do the things I should.
Jesus loves me when I'm bad,
But it makes Him very sad.

CHORUS

Jesus loves me, He who died,
Heaven's gates to open wide.
He will wash away my sins,
Let His little child come in.

CHORUS

26. JESUS LOVES THE LITTLE CHILDREN

Jesus loves the little children,
All the children of the world,
Red and yellow, black and white,
They are precious in his sight,
Jesus loves the little children
of the world.

2. Jesus died for all the children...
3. Jesus rose for all the children...
4. Jesus lives for all the children...

27. LORD GOD ALMIGHTY

Lord, God Almighty (echo)
Gonna sing, sing, sing for you (echo)
(repeat both lines)
Gonna work and pray
And sing every day for you
(repeat both lines)

2. Preach
3. Fight
4. Die

28. MY GOD IS SO BIG

My God is so big, so strong and so mighty,
There's nothing my God cannot do.
My God is so big, so strong and so mighty,
There's nothing my God cannot do.
The mountains are His, the valleys are His,
And the stars are His handiwork too.
My God is so big, so strong and so mighty,
There's nothing my God cannot do.

29. MY LORD, HE DONE DONE

CHORUS:
My Lord (my Lord), He done, done,
(repeat twice)
He done, done what He said He'd do.

2. He done give us Jesus...
3. He done give us love...
4. He done give us joy...
5. He done give us hope...

30. OH BE CAREFUL

Oh be careful little eyes what you see!
Oh be careful little eyes what you see!
There's a Father up above
looking down with tender love, so
Be careful little eyes what you see.

2. Oh be careful little ears what you hear!
3. Oh be careful little mouth what you say!
4. Oh be careful little hands what you touch!

31. OH, HOW I LOVE JESUS

Oh, (name), do you love Jesus?
(reply) Oh, yes I love Jesus
Are you sure you love Jesus?
(reply) Yes, I'm sure I love Jesus
Tell us why you love Jesus
(reply) This is why I love Jesus
Because he first loved me!

32. PEACE LIKE A RIVER

I've got peace like a river,
I've got peace like a river,
I've got peace like a river,
In my soul!—YAHOO!!
I've got peace like a river,
I've got peace like a river,
I've got peace like a river,
In my soul!—YAHOO!!

2. I've got love like an ocean,
3. I've got joy like a fountain,
4. I've got peace like a river,
   I've got love like an ocean,
   I've got joy like a fountain,
   In my soul!—YAHOO!!

(repeat)

33. PETER, JAMES AND JOHN

Peter James and John in a sailboat!
(repeat twice)
Out on the deep blue sea!
Cast their nets, but caught no fishes
(repeat twice)
Out on the deep blue sea

Along came Jesus walking on the seashore
(repeat twice)
Out on the deep blue sea

Cast your nets on the other side!
(Repeat twice)
Out on the deep blue sea

Caught their nets so full of fishes
(repeat three times)
Out of the deep blue sea!

Jesus said you'll fish for men
(repeat twice)
so men will come to me

34. ROLL THE GOSPEL CHARIOT

Roll the gospel chariot along. (repeattwice)
And we won't tag along behind.

If our brother's in the way we will
stop and pick him up (repeat twice)
And we won't tag along behind.

If the Devil's in the way, we will
roll right over him (repeat twice)
And we won't tag along behind

35. SEA OF GALILEE

There's a sea of Galilee.
There's a sea of Galilee.
There's a sea, there's a sea.
There's a sea of Galilee.

There's a boat in the sea of Galilee.
There's a boat in the sea of Galilee.
There's a boat, there's a boat,
There's a boat in the sea of Galilee.

3. There are men in the boat on the sea of Galilee.
4. There are hands on the men in the boat on the sea of Galilee.
5. There are nets in the hands of the men in the boat on the sea of Galilee.
6. There are fish in the nets in the hands of the men in the boat on the sea of Galilee.
7. There are many, many fish in the nets in the hands of the men in the boat on the sea of Galilee.

36. SHOW ME THE WAY

The blind man sat by the road and he cried
(repeat twice)
he cried oh oh oh show me the way,
show me the way, show me the way,
the way to go home.
The woman sat by the well and she cried
(repeat twice)
she cried oh oh oh show me the way,
show me the way, show me the way,
the way to go home.

Jesus hung on the cross and he died
(repeat twice)
He cried oh, I am the way,
I am the way, I am the way,
the way to go home.

Jesus rose from the dead and He cried
(repeat twice)
He cried oh oh oh show them the way,
show them the way, show them the way,
the way to go home. Jesus.

37. TAKE THE LORD WITH YOU

You've got to take the Lord with you,
children,
Everywhere you go. (Repeat twice)

CHORUS:
In the street, in the home, on the job, all alone;
Highways, byways, highways, byways,

2. Make disciples, daily... (Repeat twice)
3. Love your brothers, daily... (Repeat twice)

38. THANK YOU FOR MAKING ME ME!

If I were a butterfly,
I'd thank you Lord for giving me wings,
and if I were a bird in a tree,
I'd thank you Father for making me sing,
and if I were a fish in the sea,
I'd wiggle and I'd squiggle and I'd giggle with glee but I just thank you Lord for making me, me.

CHORUS

Cuz you gave me a heart and you gave me a smile you gave me Jesus and you made me a child and I just thank you Lord for making me, me.
If I were an elephant,
I'd thank you Lord for raising my trunk
and if I were a kangaroo
I'd hop right up to you
and if I were an octopus
I'd thank you Lord for my good looks!
but I thank you Lord for making me, me.

CHORUS

39. THANK YOU, LORD

Thank you, Lord, for loving me.
And thank you, Lord, for blessing me,
And thank you, Lord, for making me whole and saving my soul.

CHORUS:
I want to thank you, Lord, for loving me.
Thank you, Lord, for saving my soul.

Let us all with one accord
Sing praises to Christ the Lord.
Let us all unite in song to praise Him all day long.

CHORUS

Please reveal your will for me
So I can serve you for eternity.
Use my life in every way.
Take hold of it today.

CHORUS

40. THE CHRISTIAN JUBILEE

Sing me up, (echo) for the Christian Jubilee.
Write my name (echo) on the roll.
I've been changed (echo) since the Lord has lifted me.
Oh I want to be ready, ready when Jesus comes.

41. THE GOSPEL

Love, love, love, love,
The Gospel in one word is love.
Love your neighbor as your brother.
Love, love, love.

Peace, peace, peace, peace,
The Gospel in one word is peace.
Peace that passes all understanding.
Peace, peace, peace.

Joy, joy, joy, joy,
The Gospel in one word is joy.
Joy that fills to overflowing.
Joy, joy, joy.

42. THE LORD IS MY SHEPHERD

The Lord is my shepherd
I'll walk with Him always
He leads through green pastures
I'll walk with Him always
Always, always
I'll walk with Him always
Always, always
I'll walk with Him always.

43. THE NEW TESTAMENT SONG

Matthew, Mark, Luke, John
Acts and the letter to the Romans
First and Second Corinthians
Galatians and Ephesians
Philippians, Colossians
First and Second Thessalonians
First and Second Timothy
Titus and Philemon
Hebrews, James
First and Second Peter
First and Second and Third John
Jude and Revelation

44. THIS LITTLE LIGHT OF MINE

This little light of mine, I'm gonna let it shine. (repeat twice)
Let it shine, let it shine, let it shine oh yeah!

2. When I'm with my parents ...
3. When I'm at the playground...
4. All around my neighborhood...
5. Let it shine till Jesus comes...
6. Hide it under a bushel, NO!
7. Won't let Satan blow it out...

45. THIS IS THE DAY

This is the day, this is the day,
That the Lord has made,
That the Lord has made.
We will rejoice, we will rejoice,
And be glad in it, and be glad in it.
This is the day that the Lord has made,
We will rejoice and be glad in it.
This is the day, this is the day
That the Lord has made.

46. WE ARE SOLDIERS IN THE ARMY

CHORUS
We are soldiers. We're in the army,
We've gotta fight (u-hu-hu)
We've gotta fight.
We've gotta hold up the blood stained banner;
We've gotta hold it up until we die.

You know ________*(repeat)*, he(she) was a soldier,
He put his hand to the gospel plow (yes he did);
Well one day he got old, he couldn't fight anymore, He had to stand up and fight anyhow.

47. WE SHALL OVERCOME

We shall overcome, We shall overcome,
We shall overcome today;
O, deep in my heart, I do believe, We shall overcome today.

The Lord will see us through,
The Lord will see us through,
The Lord will see us through today;
O, deep in my heart, I do believe, The Lord will see us through today.

It's on to victory!
It's on to victory!
It's on to victory, today!
O, deep in my heart, I do believe,
It's on to victory today!

48. WHISPER A PRAYER

Whisper a prayer in the morning.
Whisper a prayer at noon.
Whisper a prayer in the evening
To keep your heart in tune.

God answers prayers in the morning.
God answers prayers at noon.
God answers in the evening
So keep your heart in tune.

Jesus may come in the morning.
Jesus may come at noon.
Jesus may come in the evening
So keep your heart in tune.

49. WHOSE SIDE ARE YOU LIVING ON?

Tell me whose side are you living on?
(all) I'm living on the Lord's side.
(repeat both lines)

CHORUS:
I'm livin', I'm livin', I'm livin', I'm livin',
I'm livin' on the Lord's side.
(repeat)
2. Singing
3. Praying
4. Loving
5. Serving, etc...

50. WISE MAN

The wise man built his house upon the rock
(repeat twice)
and the rain came tumbling down. OH!

The rains came down and the floods came up!
(repeat twice)
and the wise man's house stood firm! BUT...

The foolish man built his house upon the sand
(repeat twice)
and the rain came tumbling down. OH!

The rains came down and the floods came up!
(repeat twice)
and the foolish man's house went
SPLAT!!

SO...Build your house upon the Lord Jesus
Christ (repeat twice)
and your house will stand firm!

Ten Ways to Build Relationships with Your Neighbors

by Stan and Betty Morehead

1. Volunteer to baby-sit, especially for those who do not have family in the area.

2. Host dessert parties, pot-luck dinners and open house parties.

3. Canvas the neighborhood for community projects: American Heart Association, etc.

4. Give flowers to the widows on Valentine's Day.

5. Be the first to welcome a new move-in. Give them a map of the neighborhood showing the names of other residents. Find out what other information you can provide to make their transition smooth.

6. Use local businesses and develop the relationships.

7. Give positive feedback to town officials: police, librarians, school teachers.

8. Volunteer at schools, especially unwanted jobs (cleaning up after late night graduation party, etc.)

9. Take walks at times when neighbors are likely to be outside. Stop and chat with them.

10. Shovel or snowblow the neighbors' driveway, rake leaves for the elderly.

Twelve Ways to Keep the Holidays Spiritual and Joyful

1. **Matthew 6:33** - Seek the kingdom of God and his righteousness first. Decide you will not let anything distract you from great time with God every day. It is a challenging time of the year. You will need this more than ever. Every day you need to hear spiritual wisdom. Every day you need a close walk with God. Make plans and follow through.

2. **Psalm 119:97, 99**. Meditate on great passages that deal with situations you are going to be in, challenges you will face. Keep them ever before you. (Example: James 3:17-18).

3. **Hebrews 3:12** - Encourage one another daily. Don't think for a minute that you will not need this during the holidays. (Don't think for a minute the enemy takes two weeks off and goes to visit his nephew Wormwood.) Talk things over with your discipleship partner and get a plan. Discuss the kind of encouragement that will be needed and how to make it happen.

4. **Matthew 5:14-16** - Let your light shine! Be different. Preach a sermon with your life. Show love, say "I love you," be a servant, be thankful, be kind, be unselfish.

5. **Colossians 3:13** – Resolve conflicts, ask for forgiveness, practice forgiveness. There will be bumps. Some will hurt. But confess or forgive and get back on track. *Romans 12:18: "If it is possible, as far as it depends on you, live at peace with everyone."*

6. **Proverbs 19:20** — Get advice about difficult situations, long standing problems. If you are leaving town, get advice about how long to be gone, about how to get with disciples in other cities. If you have never opened up your various family dynamics and received input, make this a priority.

7. **Colossians 4:5** —Be wise in the way you act toward outsiders; make the most of every opportunity. Realize with family, it usually takes time. Plant and water seeds, but don't try to force them to grow overnight. Watch out that you don't come across as self-righteous or spiritually arrogant.

8. **Romans 12:1-2**—be alert to how the world will try to squeeze you into its mold (with family, office parties, or just in buying what everybody else is buying).

9. **Ephesians 4:22**—watch out for the *re-appearance* of your old self. Often when we go back into situations with family we revert to old ways that we thought we had put off. Think about these things in advance. Write them down. Pray about them. Ask others to pray about them. Be proactive. Outsmart Satan.

10. **Ephesians 6:4**—Parents, have great time with your own family. Don't exasperate. Build memories. Teach them with words and with your life. Deal with discipline issues firmly, but don't let it cause you to lose your joy. Note: Think through your holiday schedule in advance. Balance the time between various needs. Give to others, but make sure you get time with your immediate family. Communicate in advance so expectations will be clear.

11. **2 Corinthians 6:13**—"open wide your hearts." If the holidays bring up painful issues for you (and they do for many), open your heart up to someone. Talk it through. Get perspective. Get help from the Scriptures. Some will not be able to be with their families. You may feel down about that. That's normal. But work it through. God's plan is for you to be a light this season not a pall on the party.

12. **Psalm 68:6, Proverbs 14:31**—Don't forget the lonely and the poor. Reach out and share with those in need.

Fifteen Ideas for Singles' Households

Be very careful then, how you live—not as unwise but as wise, making the most of every opportunity, because the days are evil.
EPHESIANS 5 :13

1. Think of being in a household not just in a "situation." Get advice about who should lead and be responsible for the spirituality of the household.

2. Make the place you live a special place—more than a place just to eat and sleep. Brothers, especially take note.

3. Build *family* through sharing, service, submission and sacrifice.

4. Be devoted to unity. While the potential for disunity abounds, single households also provide an unparalleled opportunity for teaching, learning and practicing biblical unity.

5. Make a commitment to eat meals together.

6. Organize, plan and open your house to visitors on a regular basis. (Read and discuss together the *Fine Art of Hospitality* also published by DPI).

7. Have a designated "family night." Read the Bible together. Sing together. Pray together. Help the poor together. Evangelize together.

8. Deal righteously with all financial obligations and commitments.

9. Don't be conflict avoiders. Deal with differences and feelings openly and prayerfully. Talk things out.

10. Confess your sins to one another. Forgive one another.

11. Build relationships with marrieds, marrieds with kids, single moms and their kids. Reach out, invite them into your home.

12. Create a list of household chores. Divvy them up and hold each other accountable. Switch weekly or monthly.

13. Be a good neighbor. Don't let trash pile up. Shovel snow off the walks. Park legally. Shine!

14. Serve other households. Single sisters, help the single brothers make their homes special, make them meals, give them tips on decorating, ask if they need any household things. Single brothers, serve your single sisters, change that light fixture, paint their new apartment, shovel their walk after a snow, ask if they need anything done around the house.

15. Be sacrificial with your home. Make your home a haven and a shelter in the storm. Put up someone in need—disciples looking for an apartment, relatives of disciples in town for a wedding, etc.

Ten Passages You May Not Use Enough

1. Titus 3:4-5
But when the kindness and love of God our Savior appeared, he saved us, not because of righteous things we had done, but because of his mercy. He saved us through the washing of rebirth and renewal by the Holy Spirit…

2. Romans 8:1
Therefore, there is now no condemnation for those who are in Christ Jesus…

3. Luke 6:27-31
"But I tell you who hear me: Love your enemies, do good to those who hate you, bless those who curse you, pray for those who mistreat you. If someone strikes you on one cheek, turn to him the other also. If someone takes your cloak, do not stop him from taking your tunic. Give to everyone who asks you, and if anyone takes what belongs to you, do not demand it back. Do to others as you would have them do to you."

4. 1 Peter 2:13-17
Submit yourselves for the Lord's sake to every authority instituted among men: whether to the king, as the supreme authority, or to governors, who are sent by him to punish those who do wrong and to commend those who do right. For it is God's will that by doing good you should silence the ignorant talk of foolish men. Live as free men, but do not use your freedom as a cover-up for evil; live as servants of God. Show proper respect to everyone: Love the brotherhood of believers, fear God, honor the king.

5. Ephesians 4:1-3
As a prisoner for the Lord, then, I urge you to live a life worthy of the calling you have received. Be completely humble and gentle; be patient, bearing with one another in love. Make every effort to keep the unity of the Spirit through the bond of peace.

6. Matthew 20:26-28
Not so with you. Instead, whoever wants to become great among you must be your servant, and whoever wants to be first must be your slave— just as the Son of Man did not come to be served, but to serve, and to give his life as a ransom for many."

7. Luke 17:10
So you also, when you have done everything you were told to do, should say, 'We are unworthy servants; we have only done our duty.' "

8. Jude 1:22
Be merciful to those who doubt;

9. Luke 9:49-50
"Master," said John, "we saw a man driving out demons in your name and we tried to stop him, because he is not one of us."
"Do not stop him," Jesus said, "for whoever is not against you is for you."

10. Galatians 3:3
Are you so foolish? After beginning with the Spirit, are you now trying to attain your goal by human effort?

Ten Thoughts to Begin a Day

Taken from
"Fifty Power Thoughts,"
Mind Change:
The Overcomer's Handbook
by Thomas A. Jones

1

In every situation there is a right and spiritual way to think.

It may take me some time to find it.
It may take some discipline to embrace it.
But it is always there,
and it is always best.
It is always the key to overcoming
any challenge.

PHILIPPIANS 1:27
EPHESIANS 5:20

2

God is in control. Today. . .tomorrow. . .forever. God is God.

Nothing is outside his sovereignty.
He cannot lose control.
He is never surprised or unprepared.
God never asks,
"What are we going to do now?"

PSALM 2:2-6
PSALM 90:2
ISAIAH 50:7

3

God will provide.

No matter what the need. He cares.
He allows us to have needs.
He sees our needs.
He meets them all.

ISAIAH 58:11
MATTHEW 6:28-34
PHILIPPIANS 4:19

4

Accept whatever comes. . . with faith.

Disappointment? Faith.
Unfairness? Faith.
Fear? Faith.
Temptation? Faith.
Opportunity? Faith.
Victory? Faith.

HEBREWS 11:13-16
1 JOHN 5:4

5

Relax. Your God reigns.

PSALM 47:8
ISAIAH 52:7

6

God is with you, mighty warrior.

Who me? Yes you!
But I am the weakest of the weak.
So what. God loves to be with the weak.
Remember Gideon.

JUDGES 6

7

Be thankful. Laugh. Sing. Trust God.

Apply this today.
Apply it every day.
Yes, even with what is happening today.
Don't let any new development stop you.

1 THESSALONIANS 5:16-18
PROVERBS 31:25
PSALM 146:7
JOHN 14:1

8

In *all* things God works for your good.

No exceptions and no lapses.
Even in what happened yesterday.
Even in something that caused great pain.
Even in something that dashed your hopes.
All things means *all* things.

ROMANS 8:28

9

No complaining! None!

Not about anyone.
Not about anything.
Address problems and find solutions
but don't complain.

PHILIPPIANS 2:13
PHILIPPIANS 4:8-9
1 PETER 4:9

10

He arose!

That changes everything!
How different does your problem look
when placed at the mouth of
the empty tomb?

ROMANS 8:11
1 CORINTHIANS 15:12-20
1 PETER 3:21-22

PART FOUR

•Planning and Evaluation•

Your Ten Deepest Convictions

Those things you believe most deeply.
Those convictions that most impact your life.

1.____

____

2.____

____

3.____

____

4.____

____

5.____

____

6.____

____

7.____

____

8.____

____

9.____

____

10.____

____

Personal Mission Statement

Fifty Things You Want to Do Before You Die

(from the mundane to the sublime)

1.____________________

2.____________________

3.____________________

4.____________________

5.____________________

6.____________________

7.____________________

8.____________________

9.____________________

10.____________________

11.____________________

12.____________________

13.____________________

14.____________________

15.____________________

16.____________________

17.____________________

18.____________________

19.____________________

20.____________________

21.____________________

22.____________________

23.____________________

24.____________________

25.__________

26.__________

27.__________

28.__________

29.__________

30.__________

31.__________

32.__________

33.__________

34.__________

35.__________

36.__________

37.__________

38.__________

39.__________

40.__________

41.__________

42.__________

43.__________

44.__________

45.__________

46.__________

47.__________

48.__________

49.__________

50.__________

Chapters in Your Autobiography

If you were to write an autobiography what would be ten chapter titles?

1.____

2.____

3.____

4.____

5.____

6.____

7.____

8.____

9.____

10._______________________________________

Ten Sins God Has Forgiven in Your Life

(Sure the list could be much longer!)

1.____

2.____

3.____

4.____

5.____

6.____

7.____

8.____

9.____

10._______________________________________

Ten Things You Most Appreciate About God

1.______________________________
2.______________________________
3.______________________________
4.______________________________
5.______________________________
6.______________________________
7.______________________________
8.______________________________
9.______________________________
10.______________________________

Ten Things You Most Appreciate About Your Spouse or Your Best Friend

1.______________________________
2.______________________________
3.______________________________
4.______________________________
5.______________________________
6.______________________________
7.______________________________
8.______________________________
9.______________________________
10.______________________________

Ten Reasons to Be Joyful and Thankful in *All* Circumstances

1. ____________________
2. ____________________
3. ____________________
4. ____________________
5. ____________________
6. ____________________
7. ____________________
8. ____________________
9. ____________________
10. ____________________

Ten People Who Are Great Examples in Your Life

1. Of faith____________________
2. Of love____________________
3. Of perseverance____________________
4. Of joy____________________
5. Of boldness____________________
6. Of integrity____________________
7. Of kindness____________________
8. Of patience____________________
9. Of openness____________________
10. Of humility____________________

Ten People You Want to Bring to Christ

1.______________________________

2.______________________________

3.______________________________

4.______________________________

5.______________________________

6.______________________________

7.______________________________

8.______________________________

9.______________________________

10.______________________________

Ten People Who Have Left God but Can Be Brought Back

1.______________________________

2.______________________________

3.______________________________

4.______________________________

5.______________________________

6.______________________________

7.______________________________

8.______________________________

9.______________________________

10.______________________________

Ten Old Friends That You Need to Call

1. ______________________________
2. ______________________________
3. ______________________________
4. ______________________________
5. ______________________________
6. ______________________________
7. ______________________________
8. ______________________________
9. ______________________________
10. ______________________________

Ten Books That You Want to Read

1. ______________________________
2. ______________________________
3. ______________________________
4. ______________________________
5. ______________________________
6. ______________________________
7. ______________________________
8. ______________________________
9. ______________________________
10. ______________________________

Ten Things You Want Said About You When You Die

1. ______________________________

2. ______________________________

3. ______________________________

4. ______________________________

5. ______________________________

6. ______________________________

7. ______________________________

8. ______________________________

9. ______________________________

10. ______________________________

Permission to Photocopy

Discipleship Publications International grants permission for the following pages to be photocopied and distributed to others when being used in settings where no charge is being made for the materials.

118	Recommended Reading List
126-129	You Made the Right Decision
133-134	A Dozen Passages to Help in Your Ministry
140-142	Forty Scriptures to Build Character in Children
150-159	Fifty Songs for Family Devotionals
168-177	Part Four: Planning and Evaluation—all pages

Who Are We?

Discipleship Publications International (DPI) began publishing in 1993. We are a non-profit Christian publisher affiliated with the International Churches of Christ, committed to publishing and distributing materials that honor God, lift up Jesus Christ and show how his message practically applies to all areas of life. We have a deep conviction that no one changes life like Jesus and that the implementation of his teaching will revolutionize any life, any marriage, any family and any singles household.

Since our beginning we have published more than 75 titles; plus we have produced a number of important, spiritual audio products. More than one million volumes have been printed, and our works have been translated into more than a dozen languages—international is not just a part of our name! Our books are shipped regularly to every inhabited continent.

To see a more detailed description of our works, find us on the World Wide Web at www.dpibooks.com. You can order books by calling 1-888-DPI-BOOK twenty-four hours a day. From outside the US, call 781-937-3883, ext. 231 during Boston-area business hours.

We appreciate the hundreds of comments we have received from readers. We would love to hear from you. Here are other ways to get in touch:

Mail: DPI, One Merrill St., Woburn, MA 01801
E-mail: dpibooks@icoc.org

Find us on the World Wide Web

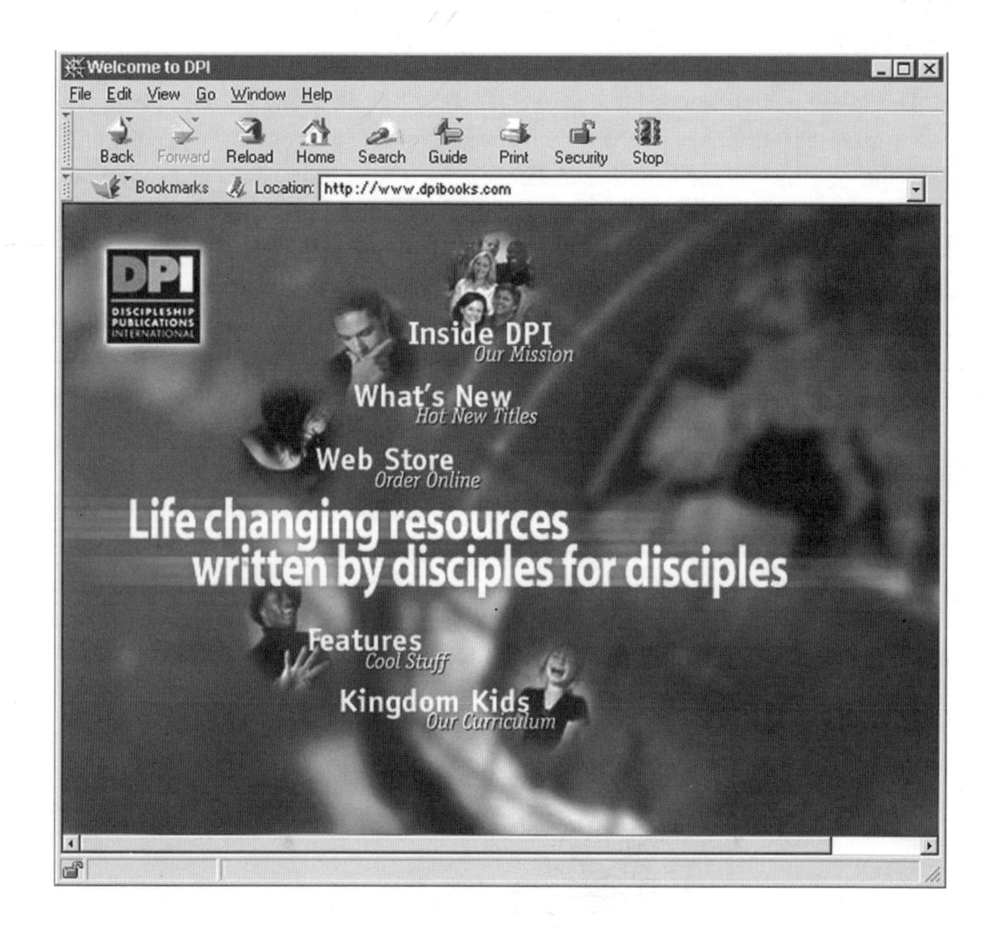

www.dpibooks.com
1-888-DPI-BOOK
outside US: 781-937-3883 x231